Practical Theology
for Church Diversity

Practical Theology for Church Diversity

A Guide for Clergy and Congregations

KEN J. WALDEN

Foreword by
VERGEL L. LATTIMORE III

CASCADE *Books* · Eugene, Oregon

PRACTICAL THEOLOGY FOR CHURCH DIVERSITY
A Guide for Clergy and Congregations

Cascade Books
An Imprint of Wipf and Stock Publishers
199 W. 8th Ave., Suite 3
Eugene, OR 97401

www.wipfandstock.com

ISBN 13: 978-1-62032-379-3

Cataloging-in-Publication data:

Walden, Kenny J.

Practical theology for church diversity : a guide for clergy and congregations / Ken J. Walden ; foreword by Vergel L. Lattimore III

xiv + 132 p. ; 22 cm. —Includes bibliographical references.

ISBN 13: 978-1-62032-379-3

1. Multiculturalism—Religious aspects—Christianity. 2. Race relations—Religious aspects—Christianity. 3. Pastoral counseling—Cross-cultural studies. I. Lattimore III, Vergel L. II. Title.

BV4468 .W35 2015

Manufactured in the U.S.A.

Dedicated to Michelle

Contents

Foreword

IT IS A RARE occurrence in academia, particularly in theological education, that we encounter a professor who possesses the keen eyes of ethnographic sensitivity, the depth of pastoral experience, and the broad affective understanding (dynamic empathy) for congregational ministry. This rich, enlightening volume by Dr. Walden is fascinatingly instructive for its unique treatment of a subject matter that is vital to an understanding of pastoral ministry from a systematic theological perspective and from a sociological study of religion perspective.

Diversity and authentic race relations continue to be a growing edge for majority and non-majority church denominations. Dr. Walden's cogent and expansive advisory prods local congregational pastors and denominational executives/supervisors to intentionally and creatively extend authentic ministry beyond racial and cultural divides that exist in many communities. Moreover, the author offers more than theoretical reflection—he provides tested proofs and lived perspectives based on his effective multicultural training, interactions, and pastoral experiences. His orderly and detailed suggestions reflect a multilevel approach to encountering cultural difference that is in service to spiritual collaboration.

From a theological perspective, Dr. Walden essentially presents a practical training manual for cross-racial ministry readiness, planning, exploration, delivery, and evaluation. The process of multicultural ministry is usefully portrayed as starting with self-awareness and extending to community-building. He advises that pastors and lay leaders should be fully aware of stereotypes and false assumptions about "others" that tend to prevent or limit genuine cross-cultural exchanges.

Dr. Walden's work is a testament to faithful action steps for basic cultural bridge-building. He addresses the limitations that have been gleaned from true lessons learned from his professional affiliations—ordained pastor, military chaplain, and seminary professor. This book will prove essential for parish pastors, instructional chaplains, and other pastoral caregivers who are called and committed to a caring ministry with members of the human family, especially those communities and groups that we have only speculated about as we travel through their streets or pass through their communities. This book is also cutting-edge for the seminary student who has visions of ministering with more than one cultural, ethnic, or racial group within the body of Christ.

Vergel L. Lattimore III

President and Professor of
Pastoral Psychology and Counseling
Brigadier General, USAF (Retired)
Hood Theological Seminary
Salisbury, North Carolina

Introduction

WHY IS THIS BOOK needed? Why is church diversity becoming an important challenge to face theologically? Why do we need a practical theology to deal with church diversity?

The world is becoming increasingly diverse, with the United States one of the most diverse countries on the planet. I have pastoral colleagues of different ethnicities—African American, African, Caucasian, Chinese American, Korean American, Korean, Japanese American, Japanese, Filipino, and Samoan—who are in cross-racial pastoral ministry. My colleagues and I have come to a consensus that various institutions—congregations, denominations, faith communities, colleges, universities, seminaries, and theological programs—often discuss the importance of church diversity, however they seldom have a pragmatic contemporary model to utilize as a resource. Simply put, church diversity *matters [just an assertion at this point. Why does it matter?]*. This book applies practical theological inquiries and methods to explore church diversity's past and present and well as its possibilities in the future.

A cross-racial pastoral ministry occurs when a clergyperson pastors a congregation consisting predominantly of an ethnicity different than her own. Upon my graduation with a Master of Divinity degree from Duke Divinity School, I accepted a cross-racial pastoral ministry assignment. As a newly minted MDiv, I did not realize that cross-racial pastoral ministry and multicultural ministry would become a major component in my life. In my fourth pastoral assignment, I accepted another cross-racial pastoral ministry assignment.

Generally, a multicultural ministry occurs when a clergyperson pastors a congregation that consists of multiple ethnicities. By God's grace, I experienced amazing ministry moments at all of my pastoral assignments. However, I quickly recognized cross-racial pastoral ministry and multicultural ministry as wonderfully complex for many reasons that will be explored in the chapters of this book.

This book offers a pragmatic approach in the form of a practical theology for church diversity, with a special emphasis on cross-racial pastoral ministry and multicultural ministry, among other aspects. As a *practical theologian* within the context of church diversity, I *analyze the interactions* (including inconsistencies) *between beliefs and actions in order to create strategies that can enhance congregations on a horizon of faith.*[1] Following the tradition of practical theology, this book identifies a specific problem, explores major contributing factors of the problem, and then offers some solutions to the problem.

Chapter 1 discusses the "big picture" regarding church diversity in the United States and identifies patterns within the American religious landscape. It elaborates on the unique virtues of cross-racial pastoral ministry and multicultural ministry in relation to God.

Chapter 2 highlights the importance for incoming pastors of preparing for a cross-racial pastoral ministry through various exercises that include not only self-examination as it relates to race and religion, but also honest discussions with mentors and especially with close family members who will be directly involved in the transition. This chapter recommends inserting a practical theology in the process of preparation through various means: conversations with church committees, questions to long-term members, and spiritual exercises such as prayer.

Chapter 3 explains the significance of the welcome introduction between the clergyperson and the church community. It is

---

1. Pattison, *Challenge of Practical Theology,* 197.

essential for both parties to apply a practical theology in laying a solid foundation at the beginning through team-building activities and "get to know you" events, so that negative stereotypes and unhelpful prejudices can start to be dispelled and managed by personal interactions.

Chapter 4 describes how collaborations between the clergy and the congregation should occur with great intentionality and thoughtfulness in the midst of cultural differences. This chapter reveals how applying a practical theology in the process of collaboration can give glory to God.

Chapter 5 discloses several widespread challenges that occur during church diversity. Following a practical theology method, this chapter provides insightful, critically assembled evidence of the common challenges that exist within cross-racial pastoral ministry and multicultural ministry, such as miscommunication, territorial conflict, and identity crisis.

Chapter 6 makes recommendations on how to respond to specific challenges that may exist in church diversity, and suggests various "extra mile" actions that clergy and congregations can take in order to go beyond the surface, minimum, or window dressing. Though extra miles may require more work for the clergy and the congregation alike, this chapter offers a practical theology that includes communication techniques, church leadership diplomacy methods, and activities to harness the necessary skills for diversity to thrive in sacred spaces and to develop a thriving church community.

Practical theologians mean to redefine power as God-given, innate authority.[2] As a practical theologian, I acknowledge the power of walls of division within congregational life based upon prejudicial practices. As a practical theologian, I also acknowledge the possibilities of God's miraculous power working through Christians engaging strategically to build bridges. I invite you to join me!

2. Stevenson-Moessner, *Prelude to Practical Theology*, 49.

1
The Big Picture

GETTING A BIG PICTURE of the challenge of diversity for congregations and their leaders often involves questions about the many shapes, forms, and sizes of diverse communities. A practical theology examination helps faith communities encounter their challenges in a candid yet curative manner—meaning, this book not only highlights some problems but also spends a substantial amount of time on possible solutions. A mentor of mine once told me, "Most people are too close to the frame of their lives to see the big picture." I have tried to pass the same words of wisdom on to other people, especially church folk. What is the big picture for your life? What do you currently see? What is the big picture for your church community? Again, what do you currently see? Without a big picture that includes aspects of difference, united in harmonious ways, church communities can become distracted, get lost, or lose sight of what is most important. With respect to church diversity, too often people forget the following:

1. Their church is not the only faith community in their geographical region.

2. They are not the only members of their church.

3. They are not the only members capable of a leadership position.

4. Their personal actions often have public consequences within their church community.

5. Their church community's actions often have repercussions within their local community.

6. The local community pays attention to the church community.

7. The Christian community is much bigger than any one church community.

Your big picture of church diversity for your faith community should facilitate ways of being that involve intentional steps of change that can be accessed through practical theology. Aspects of practical theology that help distinguish it from other theologies or disciplines include the following: it is *contextual and situationally related, sociopolitically aware and committed, experiential,* and *analytical and constructive.*[1]

How wide is your congregation's vision? Church leaders must realize the magnitude of their influence in order to be most productive. It is no coincidence that people are drawn to congregations that have solid leadership, whether it be pastoral or lay leadership. It is important for church folks to provide stable leadership in order to equip God's people in an often chaotic world. There are millions of people whose lives are characterized by instability. The chapters in their lives consist of people disappointing them through such unfortunate actions as absences, insults, and other aggravations. They do not have anyone to depend on in meaningful ways. Congregations should offer a different model of leadership—a better model, a present model, a dependable model, a supportive model, a model that does not take anything or anyone for granted, because it recognizes that "we cannot assume that equality will be present in a multicultural Christian setting. . . . Operating on the basis or supposition of equality does not make it a reality."[2]

Tradition, Scripture, experience, and reason can help confirm for us that God operates in the world. People may accept or reject

1. Pattison and Woodward, "Introduction to Pastoral and Practical Theology," 14–15.

2. Rah, *Many Colors*, 124.

God's presence through God's prophet, which is often the pastor of their local church. Church diversity in the form of cross-racial pastoral ministry and multicultural ministry is a sign of people's spiritual commitment to God. Church diversity in any form is much bigger than a specific location. Parishioners' acceptance or rejection of cross-racial pastoral ministry should not be looked upon as merely dynamics between two individuals who may be clergy and church member.

It is the responsibility of clergy to realize their role in relating to all of God's children regardless of ethnicity, nationality, race, etc. Unfortunately, in the United States, as in many other nations, church leadership has not always guided faith communities toward racial cooperation or cultural inclusiveness. In truth, many African-American Christian denominations were created primarily as a response to racial discrimination. As James Cone observes, "If white Protestant churches failed to be a beacon of leadership in America's racial crisis, part of the responsibility for the failure was due to the way its leading religious spokespersons ignored race in their interpretation of the Christian faith."[3]

As they have been historically, church leaders remain (and will continue to be) a major contributing factor to the progress of church diversity. Clergy and church leaders from all ethnicities have equal responsibility to help their faith communities' progress in diversity rather than regress. Let's be honest: churches of color can be just as prejudicial as white churches. What's more, church members who consider themselves conservative, moderate, or liberal can often criticize, demean, and ostracize the "others" in their faith communities.

It is nearly impossible to enumerate all the reasons certain people do not support church diversity. Too many excuses are generated on a daily basis for what churches cannot do or what churches cannot become. Such excuses are often based upon narrow interpretations of yesteryear and numerous blind spots of the present, rather than hopeful visions or expectations for tomorrow. Most people have an inclination to seek out those who mirror

3. Cone, *Cross and the Lynching Tree*, 57.

their own thoughts, actions, and images. To look at the big picture means to focus less on what makes one feel comfortable or secure and more on what Jesus called his disciples to become. The Bible repeatedly highlights Jesus commanding his followers to look beyond themselves.

Congregations should consider the following questions regarding church diversity:

1. What does our congregation expect to be doing in the next twenty-five years?

2. How has our congregation been distracted or derailed from our plans through the years?

3. In what ways can we improve in obeying Jesus' commands, especially as regards diversity?

4. What are some reasonable steps of progress our congregation can take in the next six to nine months to enhance church diversity?

Congregations ought to expect disagreements, battles, and tension over competing interests in relation to the big picture. Many Christians have explored or expanded their approach beyond one faith tradition or congregation. Churches can no longer rely solely on their tradition to automatically sustain, increase, or help bring meaning to their membership. In fact, denominational affiliation is a decreasing factor in why people choose to invest themselves in congregational life. Average laypersons may not articulate it theologically, but most of them are demanding a practical theology approach from their church community. According to Marcel Viau, practical theology is "a discipline whose main function is to produce discourses which convey occurrences of Christian faith practice, which itself is incorporated in human experience."[4] It is best for clergy and church leaders to realize that their individual actions, rather than what are often perceived as antiquated customs, are the major contributing factors within the life of a faith community. Growing numbers of people are seeking or demanding an increasing degree

4. Viau, *Practical Theology*, 82.

of practicality from their faith community. These same people believe that practicality is the single purpose of the Christian faith community. Their desire is to see a faith in action.

Most Christians are not expecting their church community to be perfect, but they desire a sense of realness, an authentic and genuine outlook concerning their flaws while they work to become better followers of Jesus Christ. If church perfection were a requirement from potential members, then churches everywhere would have hung a "Closed" sign on their doors a long time ago. Imperfection is a natural part of the human experience; chronic low expectations are not. Too many of our church communities are plagued by chronic low expectations in relation to church diversity, which is evident by their lack of spiritual fruit. Too often, one reason for congregations' low expectations is the inability of members to speak in a candid, courageous manner to one another. This inability to communicate well may be a consequence of our in ability to love well. As Howard Clinebell observes, "Because we had human, limited parents who had human, limited parents, all of us are limited, to some degree, in our ability to love fully. Many people are severely crippled in their ability to love in growth-nurturing ways. This is the heart of their problem. To say to such a person, 'You need to love God and neighbor more,' is like shouting to a person floating on a log in mid-ocean, 'What you need is dry land!' Nothing could be truer or less helpful."[5]

Looking at church diversity's big picture entails realizing Christians' flaws and shortcomings and still accepting all persons. Most people learn how to talk with a particular accent based on what they hear in their community, to embrace a specific belief system based on what they are taught, and to mimic certain behaviors based on what they observe. People try, people fail, and people are deficient (as well as damaged) beings, due to a combination of their inheritance, environment, and experience. Nonetheless, in the face of all their natural frustrations and innate faults, Christians have the responsibility to improve.

5. Clinebell, *Basic Types of Pastoral Care*, 65.

Seeing the big picture requires working toward greater understandings of diversity—a critical assessment through a combination of participation, explanation, evaluation, and exploration of cross-racial pastoral and multicultural church experiences, on both the individual and corporate level, in order to gain insights, offer strategies, and apply new meanings to new ways of doing and being for congregational life. "Common sense is not so common," as the saying goes, for a variety of reasons related to culture, education, upbringing, assumptions, presumptions, and religion. Although many Christians and Christian churches claim to practice a philosophy, theology, and way of life that is non-prejudicial and non-racist, too often there is a huge disconnect between theory and practice pertaining to diversity issues. Younger generations especially are in need of congregations that take church diversity within religious life seriously. Church worship services and other essential events of church life are usually more segregated than football games, soccer games, and other events. That is one reason why more people, especially younger people, are choosing to participate in activities other than religious or spiritual activities, and choosing not to attend church.

It is necessary to be familiar with the diversity issues in the U.S., but it is nearly impossible to appropriately engage in cross-racial pastoral ministry or multicultural church ministry without having adequate knowledge of history. Within this context, seeing the big picture involves realizing that you are not the first in your community to work toward achieving racial reconciliation in the United States. Several individuals and communities have attempted to live out their faith through racial reconciliation, with varied results. Therefore, it is useful to know the racial history and landscape of the particular community in which your church is located. Understanding the value of this information can help you identify prospective advocates, potential adversaries, and people who simply need to be educated about the history of race relations. One of the most significant race relationships in the U.S. is that between African-Americans and Caucasians. In his book *The Cross and the Lynching Tree*, James Cone highlights a noteworthy connection between the two: "No two people in America have had more violent and loving encounters than black and white people. We were made brothers and sisters by the blood of the lynching tree, the blood of sexual union, and the blood of the cross of Jesus. No gulf between blacks and whites is too great to overcome, for our beauty is more enduring than our brutality. What God joined together, no one can tear apart."[6]

Cone accurately acknowledges the extremely intimate relations between these two groups that comprise a history, several centuries long, of affection and antagonism within the United States. Cone justly suggests that God has joined black people and white people together; God can join all ethnicities and cultures together for extraordinary purposes. Too many Christians become sidetracked and derailed from faithfully following Jesus Christ by focusing on human differences, in the smallest and broadest sense of the word. It is Christians' responsibility to foster reconciliation and celebration among various communities, especially when the groups have a history of allowing differences to create hostility between them.

I have personally observed a myriad of aggressive acts against persons considered different in a variety of contexts. Being perceived as different has to do not only with ethnicity but also with a wide range of characteristics, such as gender, culture, belief system, education, class, and profession, among others. Ethnicity tends to be one of the most visible differences, but that is not always the case. Ethnic identities become more difficult to accurately recognize with an increasing population of international residents or citizens, along with a greater percentage of biracial children from interracial relationships. What may be perceived as different may actually be more similar than originally thought. Major institutions within the U.S., including the Christian church, have a lot of catching up to do in embracing the diverse demographics by which they are usually surrounded. Often institutions such as graduate theological schools, which are supposed to equip and advance the Christian church, do not do well in discussing diversity.

6. Cone, *Cross and the Lynching Tree*, 166.

They do a much better job conveying messages to students about what to believe than how to behave. Belief, however, does not always equate to or influence behavior, regardless of the education levels or the sophistication of a community. Miguel A. De La Torre, associate professor of social ethics and director of the Justice and Peace Institute at Iliff School of Theology, in describing his search for a tenure-track position within academia, writes,

> I didn't understand how faculty searches were really conducted. I naively believed that academics functioned above and beyond any form of political dynamics. My second "problem" was that I was a person of color, and therefore on the margins of the "good-old boy" system. As much as I wanted to believe that hires were chosen solely because of the scholastic rigor demonstrated by the applicant, the truth of the matter was that even within academic settings, race and ethnicity still mattered.[7]

Graduate theological schools should be one of the primary partners with the Christian church for direction and instruction, but many have been largely silent on diversity issues within their own institutions and within the church. There is little dialogue and a lack of serious study on church diversity. Unfortunately, many graduate theological schools reflect a similar lack of diversity as the churches they are supposed to help prepare clergy to serve. That is a huge part of the Christian churches' diversity problem.

Viewing the big picture requires an examination of contributing factors that inhibit cross-racial pastoral ministry and multicultural ministry. This examination is primarily not intended to blame anyone, but instead to help envision and then implement solutions. More research is needed on church diversity. There should be research on discrimination and the causes of the lack of diversity in congregations. To be sure, the reasons that church diversity is a challenge are many and complex. In order for Christian congregations to thrive in a changing world, however, they need resources, education, and leadership. The topic of church diversity

---

7. De La Torre, *AAR Career Guide*, "Note from the Editor," para. 2.

is deserving of serious, multifaceted investments: intellectual, financial, and human capital.

In the United States, a capitalist country, financial stability is instrumental for people and communities to survive and succeed. Many persons and communities are beholden to certain individuals primarily because of financial resources. The bleak economic situation for many congregations can lead to compromising circumstances. For example, many clergy, along with other church leaders, are too afraid or unwilling to help move their faith community toward greater diversity because they sense, or are fully aware of, the negative financial consequences, some of which can easily include unemployment for the pastor or staff, departure of congregants, and a dramatic decrease in church financial offerings.

Financial aspects of congregational life are undeniably important, but I believe one of the reasons faith communities find themselves with unfavorable financial situations is a loss of passion. Most people do not get excited about funding the status quo, the "this is how we have always done it" approach. People get excited about giving their time, talent, and finances to new ventures. There are still many new ventures that have not been faithfully or successfully explored within church diversity. There needs to be a cadre of pastors and other church leaders who are willing to risk their employment, popularity, and financial security for the greater good of including all of God's creation in their faith communities.

A broad view of church diversity does not include a narrow focus on geography; for example, to suggest that only the Southeast and certain other areas have major difficulty with inclusivity is simply not true. There are challenges with church diversity all across the United States.

One summer my family and I visited an exhibition in New York City titled "Slavery in New York" that highlighted racist labor dynamics that explain some of today's inequitable realities. (Some corporations have admitted to becoming wealthy through the exploitation of the free labor of African-American slaves.) Writing about the exhibition, William B. Harrison Jr., the former CEO and chairman of JPMorgan Chase, and Louise Mirrer, the president and CEO of the New-York Historical Society, note that slavery, which we tend to identify with the South, was widespread in colonial times:

> Though conventionally thought of as a southern institution, slavery was pervasive throughout the colonies—in Connecticut, in Delaware, in Massachusetts, in Pennsylvania, in Rhode Island and elsewhere. It was especially so in New York, where it was instrumental in the city's development during its formative years. At the time of the Revolution, approximately 41 percent of the city's households had slaves and one-in-five New Yorkers were enslaved Africans. The population of enslaved people was greater in New York than any other city except Charleston, South Carolina.[8]

Similarly, when it comes to discrimination, we focus more or less exclusively on the Southern states. To be sure, Southern states have a long history of hostility between different cultures. However, other states, including a number of Northern states, also have a long history of hostility between different cultures; in some cases, they have a longer and more brutal history. It should not come as a great surprise that Southern states can presently boast more people of color as elected political officials than other states. It should also not come as much of a surprise that church diversity is not easy to implement in any one location or region in the U.S.

New York City is the largest city in the U.S., and with its large population matched by its diversity, it is one of the most diverse cities. Still and all, church communities located in New York City do not reflect this diversity. All across the city there are churches that are predominantly African-American, predominantly Asian-American, predominantly Caucasian-American, and predominantly Hispanic-American. It is shameful that some Caucasian church members will boast of diversity on their staff by stating their custodian is a person of color. Having a person of color cleaning a predominantly Caucasian congregation's facility is not creative,

8. Mirrer and Harrison Jr., *The New York Amsterdam News* (October 7–March 5, 2005), 3.

innovative, new, or noble. Generally, there is a more diverse audience at a Broadway play than in a church's pews. It is also common to observe more diversity in the cast of a Broadway play than on a church's paid staff.

Innovative congregations embrace cross-racial pastoral ministry and multicultural ministry that go beyond simply sitting quietly in the pews. It is groundbreaking for a person of color to become the senior pastor of a predominantly Caucasian church community. It is likewise groundbreaking for a Caucasian to become the senior pastor of a predominantly African-American, Asian, or Hispanic church community.

Geographical location does not guarantee church diversity, even in a congregation with some history of inclusion located in one of the most diverse cities in the U.S. According to the *New York Times*, "The senior pastor of Riverside Church, the renowned bastion of liberal theology and social activism on the Upper West Side of Manhattan, is resigning after just nine months on the job. . . . Longtime members ascribe some of the tension to changes in the racial makeup of the 2,700-member congregation, which was once about 60 percent white and 40 percent black, and now is roughly the reverse."[9]

Riverside Church in New York City is one of many congregations that have struggled with cross-racial pastoral ministries and increased church diversity. Most congregations do not make news headlines when they grapple with issues of inclusion and the result is unsuccessful. Most congregations are not trained in cross-racial pastoral ministry and multicultural ministry. Riverside Church was newsworthy because it is one of the last places most people would imagine to have experienced this kind of controversy.

Viewing the big picture of church diversity should lead to asking serious questions that must not be narrow, insular, or inward-looking. Put another way, small questions give rise to small responses and small pictures. Cross-racial pastoral ministry should not be understood only in the context of the congregation, but with a wider range of implications and repercussions. Many

9. Vitello, "Riverside Church Pastor Resigns."

important organizations that play a significant role in the community, such as police and fire departments, the military, and hospitals, are usually required to go through diversity training to better serve people and communities. Congregations are as important as these organizations, if not more so. The following broad, outwardly oriented questions should be considered:

1. What measurable contributions has our congregation made to the surrounding community in the past five years?

   (This question is important because it helps the congregation identify concrete contributions that are not merely an assumption or an illusion.)

2. How has our congregation progressed or regressed in church diversity in the past five years? (This question is important because it helps the congregation have a more balanced view of their successes and failures.)

3. Why has our congregation decided to intentionally increase our church diversity?

   (This question is very useful because everyone should eventually be able to give a sound response that draws from a biblical, spiritual, and historical understanding.)

4. In what way(s) can our congregation improve our church diversity in the next one to three years?

   (This question should be asked because it helps move the congregation forward intentionally. The response should ultimately be written down to foster further reflection and to make the way forward more transparent.)

5. When can we get training on topics related to church diversity?

   (This question is essential to help equip the congregation for increased church diversity.)

People hurt and get hurt by other people in most organizations, including those that are supposed to offer help. Various media outlets reveal the tragic incidents, accidents, and episodes that occur in well-intended institutions such as hospices, hospitals, and schools. Congregations are no exception. Faith communities have a long-documented history of external hostility toward other peoples and internal hostility toward their own. Who cares for the victims of discrimination, whether they are pastors or lay members, in the church today? What happens to the innocent bystanders involved in these episodes? Most pastors and lay members do not receive effective care, and in some cases receive no care at all, when they suffer the bruises of discrimination either directly or indirectly within congregational life.

In May 2013 the *Washington Post* reported on the internal conflict at First Baptist Church of Washington DC, which the *Post* described as a "storied, 210-year-old" congregation: "Members say the drama that ended a few weeks ago with a 'separation agreement' between First Baptist—a prominent, mostly white church—and its first black pastor was particularly troubling. . . . Baptists, along with other mainstream American denominations, still struggle with the nation's legacy of racism and segregation, and the ministry of a black pastor to head a historically white congregation was a rare occurrence."[10] This church's membership undoubtedly experienced some distress. Similarly, the pastor who abruptly separated from the church also undoubtedly was distressed. Even during ideal pastoral transitions, it is often the case that both the church's members and the pastor experience distress. The point is that there should be more than simply reporting on congregational conflict with church diversity. There must be a greater number of persons who are highly trained and qualified to respond in compassionate ways to members and pastor alike when they experience conflict or separation from one another because of conflict. Effective intervention in a timely manner during conflict between a pastor and a congregation may prevent their separation.

The relationship between a pastor and a congregation is sacred. Why? More than just a relationship between one person and one group of people, it has an important biblical basis, from the Old Testament to the New Testament. The relationship

10. Harris and Boorstein, "Dismal Parting."

has spiritual meaning to both the faith community and the local community and can lead to worthwhile contributions to other organizations in the surrounding area. Too many communities are suffering and filled with skepticism because reliable relationships are absent, especially across lines of ethnicity.

One hundred fifty years after the 1863 Emancipation Proclamation, and less than fifty years after the 1965 Civil Rights Acts, ethnic minorities continue to fight to secure stable footing in the "land of the free." A person generally needs money to access high-quality education, health care, food, and a home. To make money, most people need a quality education, and that is one way the vicious cycle of poverty continues in too many families. Many members of ethnic minorities have gone to prison after committing a crime in order to more easily afford a home, food, health care, or an education for themselves and their family. As Paul Pryde writes,

> Recent U.S. Census Bureau statistics reveal that black families are three times as likely as whites to be poor. The number of female-headed families is on the increase, the unemployment rate for black females 18 to 19 years old is well over 50 percent; and for males in that age group, just under. By 1985, the black male unemployment rate had more than doubled that of the white male population.
>
> America's 14,731,000 business firms generated $4 trillion in 1977 (the last year for which these figures are available). The 231,203 black-owned firms accounted for less than 2 percent of this number. Most black-owned businesses operate with no full-time, paid employees, other than the owner, and fewer than 1 percent of these firms had gross receipts of more than $1 million.[11]

The lack of economic resources often relegates millions of ethnic minorities to a life of depression, contention, and crime. Too often, there is an enormous disconnect between congregational life and ethnic minorities (and Caucasians) who have found themselves engaged in crime. This disconnect is evident in the lack of outreach ministries that congregations have with jails, prisons, juvenile

---

11. Pryde, "Investing in People," 304–5.

detention centers, and foster homes, among other institutions that historically have had relationships with Christians. This disconnect adds to the difficulty of various cultures coming together. The difficulty begins when churches become increasingly insular and primarily reach out to those who supposedly mirror their way of life.

There is an abundance of communities that are publicly and privately jaundiced toward persons with certain physical features. People of faith can become devastated when they experience prejudice within a faith community. Faith communities in the form of congregations need to model a different way of living, as Clinebell has suggested: "A local church should strive to become a healing, growth-stimulating redemptive organism. The aim of the church's pastoral care program should be to develop a dynamic climate of mutual, loving, enlightened concern, which gradually leavens the whole congregation. Church administration and the small group program should be oriented toward this objective."[12] The aim of a movement toward greater church diversity should be to create places of restoration where people may heal after the headaches and heartaches caused by various forms of bigotry in the world.

Practical theology is concerned with actions, issues, and events that are of human significance in the contemporary world.[13] Practical theology for church diversity strategically seeks to help construct congregational life for all of God's children in loving and equitable ways. Most people desperately need a place of relief and respite. There are destructive ramifications to the stressors that millions of people undergo by not having access to an unconditional caring community: poor physical health, addiction to prescription drugs, and suicide, for example. People want to be *accepted* in the truest, broadest, and simplest sense of the word. Humanity is in need of acceptance in order for significant growth to occur. Howard Clinebell is correct in bringing into focus congregations' leadership objectives, which need to be more comprehensive than something like "Our congregation loves and follows Jesus Christ." A dilemma

12. Clinebell, *Basic Types of Pastoral Care*, 395.

13. Pattison and Woodward, "Introduction to Pastoral and Practical Theology," 7.

with many congregations is that they have a good idea of what they should be doing, but they have very little idea of how to actually do it. Congregations' leadership objectives need to include belief statements and action items such as those given below:

1. One of the ways we love Jesus Christ is by loving all of our brothers and sisters.

2. One of the ways we follow Jesus Christ is by helping support all of our brothers and sisters.

3. One of the ways we love our neighbors is by including all of our brothers and sisters.

IMMIGRATION

The big picture in church diversity requires congregations to examine what is going on at the local and national level, realizing that whatever is going on nationally will most likely impact them locally. The topic of immigration is becoming a strongly debated issue that is impacting various circles within the U.S. A growing number of faith communities are becoming more aware and vocal when it comes to the issue of immigration. For example, in 2009, the Evangelical Lutheran Church in America adopted a social policy resolution titled "Toward Compassionate, Just, and Wise Immigration Reform"; the resolution reads in part,

> The Evangelical Lutheran Church in America (ELCA) has a long history of helping immigrants, refugees, and asylum seekers settle in the United States and supporting fair and generous immigration policies. . . . One factor is the estimated 12 million unauthorized immigrants (close to one-half of unauthorized-immigrant households are couples with children) residing in the United States—living in the shadows, vulnerable to injustice and mistreatment, and representing a mass violation of the rule of law. . . . The ELCA recommits itself to join with

others in seeking compassionate, just, and wise immigration reform through this social policy resolution.[14]

It is a significant step forward when religious communities can make official statements on behalf of an entire denomination about the importance of accepting the stranger in the form of an immigrant. It is more significant when the denomination's congregations actually follow the official statements of inclusion regardless of ethnicity, culture, nationality, etc.[15]

Illegal immigration has exacerbated harsh living conditions in some U.S. cities, conditions that include prostitution, human trafficking, and forced manual labor with unfair wages, along with countless other crimes. Seeing the big picture of church diversity requires an honest examination of the ways in which congregations contribute to both the problems and solutions in immigration and other issues related to diversity.

In preparation for attempting to engage the problem of crimes against women during illegal immigration scenes, it is helpful to have some knowledge of where some of the women come from. For example, Kwok Pui-lan acknowledges the many unstable environments in which Asian women live and work. She suggests that before a person can intelligently participate in dialogue regarding the care of Asian women, it is important to understand their life circumstances. If Asian women's problems are ignored, then their problems will continue to affect their lives in horrific ways in years to come. She notes, "Three quarters of the world's illiterate population live in Asia. In Pakistan and Nepal, for example, 80 percent of the women are illiterate, and in some parts of India and Bangladesh, about three-quarters of the women can barely read. Poverty, family responsibilities and other hardships drive many young Asian girls and women to sell their bodies for

14. Evangelical Lutheran Church in America, "Toward Compassionate, Just, and Wise Immigration Reform."

15. For additional examples of how faith communities have engaged the topic of immigration, see Robertson, "Bishops Criticize Tough Alabama Immigration Law," and Episcopal News Service, "Episcopal Church Leaders Endorse Comprehensive Immigration Reform Legislation."

sexual services in the entertainment industries, in bars, nightclubs and discos, for example."[16]

Such are the harsh realities that place Asian women in situations that are unfathomable for average Americans. Simply encouraging these women to read the Bible as a pastoral care strategy would be ineffective, if not absurd, in many cases. More has to be done for Asian women who are being oppressed. North American Christians must not assume that all people can easily go through the same process of faith formation that they have experienced. The big picture in church diversity is alert to the harsh realities that often exist across ethnic and demographic lines.

African women and Asian women frequently live in cultures that systematically view them as being of lesser value than men. Even though the task of challenging cultural norms is often difficult and may seem impossible, the traditional use of religion, specifically Christianity, must be reversed, and it must be used instead as a vehicle for liberation. A societal change customarily requires people who have been benefiting from the traditional structure to share privileges with those who have been oppressed. In various countries and throughout history, a percentage of the privileged have resisted allowing oppressed people to be liberated, because they think that if they allowed equal access and treatment for all people they would lose their position of dominance. In reference to how most Asian women are looked upon in their culture, Pui-lan notes, "Considered a source of temptation for men, women's sexuality is looked on as power that must be guided and brought under control. Before marriage, a woman is considered the property of the father; after marriage, the husband has ownership of her body and her children. The patriarchal family institution, the churches and other religious organizations, the cultural ethos and government policies join hand in hand to keep women submissive and in their place."[17]

In many Asian societies, women currently not only have cultural norms but also governmental policies working against them.

---

16. Pui-lan, *Introducing Asian Feminist Theology*, 13.

17. Ibid., 21.

Some governmental policies contribute to a preference for male children, and so, in certain geographic regions in Asia, female children are generally despised. Asian women who are Christians are not only battling their culture but also their government. This antagonistic attitude toward women can easily enter a congregation's ethos. Christianity has been used, and in places is being used, as a vehicle of oppression against Asian women, with countless congregations (including Asian congregations) acting as participants in the injustice. Seeing the big picture, congregations in the U.S. will accept responsibility for the wrongs they committed in the past, will correct their present, and will try their best not to repeat offenses in the future. Pui-lan writes,

> Although Asian countries have become independent, there is still the colonial legacy of looking toward the West for guidance and tutoring. This is especially evident in the liturgy, organization and life of Christian churches in Asia. For a long time, theologians read Barth, Brunner, and Tillich, trying to solve theological puzzles for other contexts, with little or no relevance for Asia. This theological dependency has had devastating effects on the witness and mission of the Asian churches. After centuries of missionary effort, less than 3 per cent of the population in Asia claim to be Christian, while the majority still sees Christianity as a foreign religion, even if not condemning it as the religion of the oppressors.[18]

One of the many challenges that Asian women theologians face is creating their own theologies that will help bring about liberation for all people, including women of color. Practical theology helps with that particular endeavor.[19]

18. Ibid., 29.

19. Some sources that reveal some harsh realities of Asian women: Ebenstein, "'Missing Girls' of China and the Unintended Consequences of the One Child Policy." And Guilmoto, "Sex Ratio Imbalance in Asia: Trends, Consequences, and Policy Responses."

2

The Preparation

IT IS ESSENTIAL FOR church folk to continually prepare for becoming better disciples of Jesus Christ. Church life is not always easy or fun, but a substantial number of Christians embrace being vital members of a congregation. Church life has sacred components, but it is also susceptible to the formation of harmful characteristics; religious communities, whatever their type or denomination, are not perfect. Specifically, Christian churches are not automatically faithful, sanctified, or dedicated to God, God's Son in the person of Jesus Christ, or God's Holy Spirit. The Bible gives numerous examples, from the book of Genesis to the book of Revelation, of religious communities' confusion, reluctance, or refusal to simply obey God in the formation of their congregation. Church communities should seek to be more faithful than famous, more sanctified than successful, and more dedicated to Jesus Christ than dynamic in seeking people's applause or praise.

Preparation is equally important for clergy and churches pursuing a greater level of church diversity. This chapter will explore the importance of preparation in relation to church diversity. Through various exercises that include self-examination as it relates to race, culture, and religion, the incoming pastor should have honest discussions with mentors and especially with close family members who will be directly involved in the transition. Pastoral ministry is not easy. It requires pastors to journey with people during physical illnesses, relational fissures, and spiritual crises. The incoming pastor's situation can become more complex when there are unresolved questions, concerns, and anxiety related to race or culture. An adequate foundation through pastoral preparation should be established in order to be attentive to unresolved issues.

Preparation is essential in most endeavors when one determines to succeed in particular goals. Congregations can prepare for church diversity in the form of cross-racial ministry in various ways that include conversations with church committees, questions to long-term members, and spiritual exercises such as prayer. Many activities and accomplishments, especially those related to diversity, succeed only with great intentionality. It is unwise for any church to think that people of other cultures will just show up, attend regularly, and get involved, without the church being welcoming and offering opportunities not only for spiritual growth but also for participation at all levels of church life.

Cross-racial pastoral ministry and multicultural ministry are distinctive endeavors in twenty-first-century America. The United States progressively resembles a global village, but there are not many multicultural faith communities worshiping together on a weekly basis. Sunday morning remains the most racially segregated time in the U.S.[1] As a clergyperson, too often I hear other clergy identifying their congregations as the sole reason why they are unable to pastor a multicultural church. In order for multicultural congregations, denominations, or religious communities to become healthy and vibrant, the senior pastor must exhibit certain characteristics to be effective, such as public appreciation for cultural diversity, intentional facilitation of a balance of power fairly among the various cultures, and active research on the particular customs and needs of the mix of cultures represented within the congregation.

---

1. On the most racially segregated hour in the U.S., see Emerson and Woo, *People of the Dream*; Blake, "Why Many Americans Prefer Their Sundays Segregated"; and Winseman, "Race and Religious Leadership."

One major contributing factor to the level of church diversity is the pastor's acknowledgment and appreciation of particularities within multicultural settings. It is essential that all cultures feel valued and not ignored. Most people have a primal need to feel that they are welcomed and loved. People are three-dimensional beings with a mind, body, and soul. Effective multicultural pastoral leadership will not overlook such realities of a person's body as age, gender, and ethnicity. Elizabeth Conde-Frazier has suggested that "cultural-majority congregations need to become aware of their own cultural imperialism by making a practice of affirming the cultural heritage of each person and by teaching attitudes of respect and appreciation toward other cultures. Respect is not demonstrated by becoming blind to cultural differences; this simply renders them invisible."[2]

Pastors help lead their parishioners. Parishioners of various cultures who are members of a church should have the freedom to celebrate how God created them in relation to their respective heritage and traditions. The acknowledgments and celebrations may be variously displayed through songs, prayers, preaching styles, pastoral care, and pastoral counseling that reflect and nurture the numerous realities of multicultural ministry. If these things are prohibited, then parishioners who seek to worship God in spirit and in truth are prevented from doing so with their native or authentic expressions.

It is good to have power dynamics balanced culturally within congregations. Though there are complexities involved in trying to ensure fairness within diverse congregations, it is important to prevent one culture from displaying dominance in the church. Jason Byassee, writing in *The Christian Century*, cautions, "hiring an associate across racial lines can be a token gesture."[3] Unfair or unbalanced power dynamics do not automatically cease within religious communities simply because of a cross-racial pastoral ministry or because a congregation's membership becomes racially diverse. Congregations and pastors, especially senior pastors, need

2. Conde-Frazier, "Spiritual Journey toward Peaceful Living," 163.
3. Byassee, "Team Players," 21.

to be equally responsible and sensitive to the needs of church diversity. Most congregations are reflections of their senior pastoral leader's characteristics, especially when their senior pastor has been there for a considerable amount of time.

It is recommended for clergy and churches to have some familiarity with and appreciation for an assortment of religious customs. Many people do not want to simply imitate others' customs in order to gain entry into the life of a faith community. I have witnessed Native Americans participating in a worship service with their native clothes, music, language, and pipe-smoking. Unfamiliar with Native American customs, I asked a colleague sitting near me, "What is going on in here?" My colleague explained, "They are worshiping God in spirit and in truth. They are being authentically themselves and not what we want them to be." I am sure they appreciated a space to be authentically, spiritually themselves.

Effective pastoral leaders gather data about their soon-to-be parishioners' culture(s) before they arrive and begin their ministry. It is advantageous for the incoming pastor to be familiar with the congregation's demographics. As Emmanuel Y. Lartey writes, "Healthy 'race relations' within any community must be based on knowledge and information about the groups constituting the community. The approach to the multicultural society favored here is that of 'facts and figures' as providing the necessary tools for effective action."[4] Similarly, the congregation should be aware of their soon-to-be pastor's cultural personhood. Of course, there are a lot of variances within any single culture, race, ethnicity, nationality, or gender, among other categories of being.

Acquiring accurate information is essential for effective pastoral leadership. When the pastor lacks knowledge of the culture(s), his or her attempts may be unproductive at best; at worst, such attempts may end up being terribly harmful. Even though the pastor is responsible for leading the congregation, it is possible for congregations to harm their pastors when they have no awareness of or desire to affirm the clergyperson's being as it relates to culture, race, ethnicity, nationality, or gender.

4. Lartey, *In Living Color*, 169.

Pastors and other church leaders have important roles in helping maintain the spiritual well-being of church communities. Their responsibilities also include teaching, visitation, and other functions of their faith tradition. Not all clergypersons perceive their pastoral role in the same manner, but most would agree with the importance of their playing a supportive role during emergency situations.

Congregations need to be aware of the fact that an incoming pastor of a different ethnicity will probably be involved in their lives beyond the church walls. Cross-racial pastoral ministry and multicultural ministry require unfamiliar people to occupy intimate spaces with one another in such contexts as baptisms, counseling sessions, wedding ceremonies, hospitals, and funeral services. Wayne E. Oates defines pastoral care as "the Christian pastor's combined fortification and confrontation of persons as persons in times of both emergency crisis and developmental crisis."[5] This definition of pastoral care focuses on engaging two components of life pertaining to people's ups and downs—emergency crisis and developmental crisis—highlighting the significance of pastoral care in life. At the lowest times and the highest times, people typically need others to journey with them. Given that people of faith often consult a clergyperson, parishioners will find themselves needing their pastor, who may be a person from a different race, during a cross-racial pastoral ministry.

In preparation for cross-racial pastoral ministry, clergypersons and churches need to have a clear understanding of the words *world*, *church*, and *pastor*. The world in which we live is full of unforeseen pitfalls, mountains, and valleys that may cause extreme human suffering. Even so, this world is to be engaged by people of faith, such as Christians, who are called to be a light in the midst of gloom. Today more than ever, humanity is in need of safe persons and safe places that can offer assistance during an unexpected ordeal. The church can provide such a safe place, a community of Christians who rely on faith and who extend forgiveness, hope, grace, love, and mercy to all of God's children. Churches are better

5. Oates, *New Dimensions in Pastoral Care*, 3.

equipped to increase church diversity when they have a clear understanding of who they are, who they would like to become, and what they should be doing according to God's will. Similarly, clergy should also have a clear understanding of who they are, who they would like to become, and what they should be doing according to God's will. The pastor is the spiritual leader of the church that seeks to reflect God's principles in the world. Without a clear understanding of the words *world*, *church*, and *pastor* in the midst of church diversity, it will be nearly impossible for much work to get done. Furthermore, the understanding of those words should not be reduced to one ethnicity, nationality, or gender in order for "God's will to be done on Earth as it is in Heaven."[6]

I highly recommend clergy mentorship for all pastoral situations, especially for cross-racial pastoral ministry and multicultural ministry. My pastoral formation has been tremendously influenced in the most positive manner by mentors. I am fortunate to have qualified clergy from a variety of cultures and settings to advise me, assist me, and mentor me toward pastoral competency. Not only do I seek them, but I seriously listen to them, study their pastoral methods, and learn from them in order to increase my pastoral ability. In retrospect, a great deal of my best pastoral counsel has come from clergy with similar pastoral experiences. Simply put, my clergy mentors with experience in cross-racial pastoral ministry and multicultural ministry have been priceless to my pastoral journey. This is not to imply that laypeople do not have valuable insight, perspectives, or advice for their pastor; I am simply emphasizing the worth of the ancient practice of apprenticeship. I have also observed that apprenticeship among church members is equally important. It is wonderful when laypersons can mentor one another in various Christian roles and responsibilities.

Another important component during preparation is to have a grasp of the biblical context of church diversity. Throughout the Bible, a variety of examples of apprenticeship show the continuity

---

6. The phrase is included in the Lord's Prayer in Matt 6:10.

of God's work. A few of the classic examples are Moses and Joshua,[7] Naomi and Ruth,[8] Jesus and his disciples,[9] and Paul and Timothy.[10] Apprenticeship is one way for clergy and laity to prepare for increased efforts of church diversity. However, apprenticeship does not guarantee success on any level of church diversity. Apprenticeship may not be possible in some situations, due to geographical constraints, lack of relationships, or lack of awareness of the apprenticeship process. It is only one component in the preparation process that helps make the beautiful picture of church diversity.

BIBLICAL CONTEXT/UNDERSTANDING

It is good for clergy and churches to have some knowledge of the biblical context of diversity. Biblical knowledge can help place their situations in proper context and possibly guide them in wise directions. Increasing church diversity is an old tradition that should be seriously examined to gain insight and information, as well as to build upon, in order equip a new generation of Christians. The very beginning of the Old Testament offers aspects of diversity within God's creation, highlighting several stories of different cultures and various ethnic groups journeying through the world, encountering one another or God at specific stages in their lives. In the book of Genesis, it is made clear that we live in an exceedingly diverse world with dissimilar people, whose assorted thoughts and behaviors differ but who are all included in God's creation. Diversity is expounded upon in 1 Corinthians 12 in relation to gifts of the Spirit. This theme is also found in Rev 21:24–26, where another world/next world is described as having a characteristic of diversity. In a biblical context, diversity is acknowledged, supported, and celebrated in this world and beyond.

7. See Deut 31:7–8.

8. See Ruth 1:5–7.

9. See Matt 17:18–20; 21:5–7; and Luke 11:1–11.

10. See 1 Tim 5.

It is possible for congregations to be oblivious to their actual needs. Religious communities can be unaware of what they should be doing for themselves and other people around them. Just as a person's desires can vary from one extreme to another to the extent that their desires and their needs can become difficult to distinguish, so congregations often expend too many resources on what they desire (or desire to be doing) and too few resources on what they need (or need to be doing). Serious preparation allows time for congregations to identify desires and needs in a biblical context. William Willimon writes, "The gospel is not simply about meeting people's needs. The gospel is also a critique of our needs, an attempt to give us needs worth having. The Bible appears to have little interest in so many of the needs and desires that consume present-day North Americans."[11]

The Bible informs us that the pastor and the church should be not confined to a building, restricted to a geographical region, or regulated by customs. The pastor or shepherd has sacred responsibilities to her religious community. Sometimes, the pastor will be required to make declarations to the entire congregation, warn against sinful pitfalls, and model Christian behavior for the congregation to learn and follow.

A PASTOR'S PREPARATION FOR A CROSS-RACIAL PASTORAL MINISTRY

During my studies for my master of divinity degree at Duke University, from 1999 to 2002, I did not receive any instruction in cross-racial pastoral ministry and multicultural ministry. That was an unfortunate oversight by my graduate theological education program, because upon my graduation, I accepted a cross-racial pastoral ministry in North Carolina. Not much had changed, I found, when from 2005 to 2011 I returned to pursue my PhD in practical theology with an emphasis in pastoral care and counseling from Claremont School of Theology; again I received no

---

11. Willimon, *Pastor*, 96.

instruction in cross-racial pastoral ministry and multicultural ministry. That was equally unfortunate, because even a minimum of instruction would have been useful when I accepted a cross-racial pastoral ministry in Southern California. In addition to my faith in a powerful God, I am fortunate to have had a prayerful life, a praying wife, supportive parents, understanding in-laws, trusted mentors, and a few good friends during my pastoral journey with cross-racial pastoral ministry and multicultural ministry.

A pastor's preparation generally comes through a variety of sources, such as graduate theological education programs, apprenticeships, and on-the-job training. Unfortunately, these sources do not always adequately prepare clergy and other church leaders for church diversity. Norman Shawchuck and Roger Heuser observed that "seminaries and institutions of pastoral training are ill-equipped in curriculum development, policy making, and faculty personnel for preparing persons to 'partner' with God toward this future."[12]

An archaic theological education, a lack of apprenticeships, and unsupportive on-the-job training for church diversity make it difficult to become a competent clergyperson in contexts of church diversity in the form of cross-racial pastoral ministry and multicultural ministry. If religious communities want to become effective and relevant in an increasingly diverse world, they must think seriously about revising the ways persons are prepared to become leaders in the church.

One way clergy can prepare for a cross-racial pastoral ministry is by having a series of serious conversations with trusted individuals they usually go to for wise counsel—their mentors, pastors, counselors, or therapists. The pastor should have a safe space in which to talk with a dependable person so that honest dialogue can occur. Without any fear of judgment and disclosure, the pastor needs to feel free to discuss concerns, questions, past experiences, and expectations related to issues of race and culture within religion. The advisory sessions should be one-on-one, unless there is a training session for a class of pastors who are preparing for their cross-racial pastoral ministry. Ideally, the pastor's

12. Shawchuck and Heuser, *Leading the Congregation*, 238.

advisers should include men and women of different ethnicities, with diverse church experiences; above all, they should be prayerful people with a vision who are convinced that cross-racial pastoral ministry and multicultural ministry are essential in God's plan.

Second, a pastor's self-awareness is critical. The practice of such self-examination can occur through self-reflection, reading, and prayer during the cross-racial pastoral ministry process. The incoming pastor should engage in intercessory prayer on a daily basis, with the intent to regularly ask God's divine intervention for diversity within her church community. Pastors should reflect upon their lives in relation to race and culture within religion, because they will inevitably bring many of their own experiences and concepts with them to the church. Pastors should also read books and other literature that focuses upon cross-racial pastoral ministry and multicultural ministry in order to gain accurate perspectives and enhance pastoral tools.

QUESTIONS FOR PASTORAL SELF-EXAMINATION

1. Have any of your pastors been of a race or gender different from your own? If so, in what ways has that experience influenced you? If not, has the lack of such experience shaped your views or opinions in some way?

2. Have you ever been a member of a multicultural church? If so, in what ways has that experience influenced you? If not, has the lack of such experience shaped your views or opinions in some way?

3. Are any of your five closest friends of a different culture or gender? If so, in what ways has that experience influenced you? If not, has the lack of such experience shaped your views or opinions in some way?

4. Have you ever had a negative experience associated with race or gender? If so, in what ways has that experience influenced you? If not, has the lack of such experience shaped your views or opinions in some way?

5. What are some productive experiences and skills you possess that can help you in a cross-racial pastoral ministry?

6. What are some unproductive experiences and inabilities you possess that may not help you in a cross-racial pastoral ministry?

7. Why are you drawn to cross-racial pastoral ministry? List three to five reasons.

8. Describe your vision for cross-racial pastoral ministry.

9. What are three to five reasons you may not be drawn to a cross-racial pastoral ministry?

10. Describe your vision for a multicultural church ministry.

11. Do you have a mentor with experience in cross-racial pastoral ministry?

12. Do you have a mentor with experience in a multicultural church ministry?

13. What is your biblical/spiritual/religious understanding of your pastoral responsibilities within multicultural church ministry?

14. How do you intend to carry out your biblical/spiritual/religious understanding of your pastoral responsibilities within a cross-racial pastoral ministry?

A READING LIST FOR PASTORS

- *Pastoral Theology from a Global Perspective: A Case Study Approach*, edited by Henry S. Wilson et al. Eugene, OR: Wipf & Stock, 2005.

- *Reconciliation: Mission and Ministry in a Changing Social Order*, by Robert J. Schreiter. Maryknoll, NY: Orbis, 1992.

- *Many Faces, One Church: A Manual for Cross-Racial and Cross-Cultural Ministry*, by Earnest Lyght et al. Nashville: Abingdon, 2006.

- *Worship: Adoration and Action*, edited by D. A. Carson. Eugene, OR: Wipf and Stock, 2002.

- *How My Mind Has Changed: Essays from the Christian Century*, edited by David Heim. Eugene, OR: Cascade, 2012.

- *This Is Our Story: Free Church Women's Ministry*, edited by Janet Wootton. Peterborough, UK: Epworth, 2007.

- *Church Diversity*, by Scott Williams. Green Forest, AR: New Leaf, 2011.

- *Building a Healthy Multi-ethnic Church: Mandate, Commitments, and Practices of a Diverse Congregation*, by Mark DeYmaz. San Francisco: Jossey-Bass/Wiley, 2007.

- *Women at Worship: Interpretations of North American Diversity*, by Marjorie Procter-Smith and Janet R. Walton. Louisville: Westminster John Knox, 2004.

- *Becoming Bridges: The Spirit and Practice of Diversity*, by Gary Commins. Cambridge, MA: Cowley, 2007.

- *Becoming a Multicultural Church*, by Laurene Beth Bowers. Eugene, OR: Wipf & Stock, 2010.

A CONGREGATION'S PREPARATION FOR A CROSS-RACIAL PASTORAL MINISTRY

One way churches can prepare for a cross-racial pastoral ministry is by having a series of serious conversations with various long-term members, church committees, and other church leaders. Church members should engage in honest dialogue with one another about any apprehension they may have, as well as experiences or expectations related to cross-racial pastoral ministry. The dialogue can offer an opportunity for church members to assist one another in the process. At the very least, the church's lay leadership will gain from the dialogue a general idea of the possible strengths and weaknesses of the church body as these relate to a cross-racial pastoral ministry.

Second, churches need to exercise the spiritual practice of prayer and outreach throughout the cross-racial pastoral ministry process. Churches should intentionally engage in intercessory prayer within their congregation on a daily basis, to regularly ask God's divine intervention for racial and cultural progress within their faith community. The prayers can be printed in the worship bulletin as a liturgy, included in the form of a call to worship, as well as in other areas in the life of the congregation.

QUESTIONS FOR A CONGREGATION

1. Are any of your current chairpersons of an ethnicity different from the predominant ethnicity of the congregation? If so, in what ways has that experience impacted the congregation? If not, why not?

2. In your congregational experience, have any of your pastors ever been of a different race or gender? If so, in what ways has that experience influenced you? If not, has the lack of such experience shaped your views or opinions in some way?

3. Are any of your five closest friends of a different culture or gender? If so, in what ways has that experience influenced you? If not, has the lack of such experience shaped your views or opinions in some way?

4. What are some of your congregation's customs that may not help support a cross-racial pastoral ministry?

5. What are three to five ways your congregation can benefit from a cross-racial pastoral ministry?

6. What are some of your congregation's customs that may not help support a multicultural ministry?

7. What are three to five ways your congregation can benefit from a multicultural ministry?

8. How would you describe your vision for a multicultural ministry?

9. What are your one-year, three-year, and five-year plans for a multicultural ministry?

10. What are your one-year, three-year, and five-year plans for a cross-racial pastoral ministry?

11. Do you have a mentor with experience in cross-racial pastoral ministry?

12. Do you have a mentor with experience in multicultural ministry?

13. What is your biblical/spiritual/religious understanding of your responsibilities as a layperson within a multicultural ministry?

14. How do you intend to carry out your biblical/spiritual/religious understanding of your responsibilities as a layperson within cross-racial pastoral ministry?

A READING LIST FOR CHURCHES

- *Confirming the Pastoral Call: A Guide to Matching Candidates and Congregations*, by Joseph L. Umidi. Grand Rapids: Kregel, 2000.

- *Living in Color: Embracing God's Passion for Ethnic Diversity*, by Randy Woodley. Downers Grove, IL: InterVarsity, 2004.

- *The Post-Black and Post-White Church: Becoming the Beloved Community in a Multi-ethnic World*, by Efrem Smith. San Francisco: Jossey-Bass, 2012.

- *Burning Center, Porous Borders: The Church in a Globalized World*, by Eleazar S. Fernandez. Eugene, OR: Wipf & Stock, 2011.

- *Revisioning Christian Unity: The Global Christian Forum*, edited by Huibert van Beek. Eugene, OR: Wipf & Stock, 2009.

- *Every Tribe and Tongue: A Biblical Vision for Language in Society*, by Michael Pasquale and Nathan L. K. Bierma. Eugene, OR: Pickwick, 2011.

- *This Is Our Story: Free Church Women's Ministry*, edited by Janet Wootton. Peterborough, UK: Epworth, 2007.

- *Ethnic Blends: Mixing Diversity into Your Local Church*, by Mark DeYmaz and Harry Li. Grand Rapids: Zondervan, 2010.

- *Intentional Diversity: Creating Cross-Cultural Relationships in Your Church*, by Jim Lo. Indianapolis: Wesleyan Publishing House, 2002.

- *Dynamic Diversity: Bridging Class, Age, Race and Gender in the Church*, by Bruce Milne. Downers Grove, IL: IVP Academic, 2007.

- *Talking about Cultural Diversity in Your Church*, by Michael V. Angrosino. Lanham, MD: AltaMira, 2001.

- *Women at Worship: Interpretations of North American Diversity*, by Marjorie Procter-Smith and Janet R. Walton. Louisville: Westminster John Knox, 2004.

A CHURCH'S PREPARATION FOR MULTICULTURAL MINISTRY

Depending on the specific faith community and the geographical location, creating a multicultural ministry can be more difficult to achieve than accommodating a cross-racial pastoral ministry. A cross-racial pastoral ministry does not equate to a multicultural ministry. In the context of this book, a multicultural ministry is a faith community that has a diverse group of individuals in leadership positions in most areas of the church where major decisions occur, especially those related to finances, staffing, and worship. A cross-racial pastoral ministry can occur without a substantial amount of cultural diversity in various committees within a church.

One way a church can prepare for a multicultural ministry is to strategically envision how they sense God's call upon their faith community, and then plan accordingly. For example, when a church thinks God is calling them to a multicultural ministry, then they can identify and eventually select an ethnic person for a leadership position who is able to reflect that reality. Strategic planning should prompt action within a specific time frame; otherwise, it is simply wishful thinking.

A second way a church can prepare for a multicultural ministry is to prayerfully consider partnering with a different ethnic community. The partnership between two faith communities can take a variety of forms: a shared facility, either at different worship times or at the same worship time; shared outreach as it relates to the poor or physically ill or children's ministry; and recreational ministry as it relates to athletics and board games, to name a few.

The gender aspect is important. Clergy and lay leaders should take an honest look at their gender relations. What message(s) might they be sending about gender issues to their congregation? What message(s) might the congregation be interpreting or receiving about gender relations? Gender dynamics and gender relations have changed in a major way over the past twenty years in many Protestant denominations:

1. An increasing number of women are becoming students in seminaries.[13]

2. An increasing number of women are entering the chaplaincy in a variety of settings—hospice, hospitals, and universities, among others.[14]

3. An increasing number of women are pastoring churches.[15]

---

13. Regarding this trend, see Wiseman, "Women Increasing in Numbers at Southeastern Seminary"; "Mount Angel Seminary Educates Catholic Women."

14. On this trend, see McNerthney, "Number of Female Police Chaplains Increasing"; "ABHMS-endorsed Military Chaplain Makes Women's History."

15. Regarding this trend, see Brown, "Lead Women Pastors Make Recommendations"; Zikmund et al., "Women, Men and Styles of Clergy Leadership."

At best, religious communities have respectfully recognized male traits and female traits in complementary ways. At worst, religious communities have degraded male traits and female traits through competition. Church leadership was once an exclusive club for males only in most Christian communities. The tide is turning. Again, an increasing number of women are entering leadership roles in religious communities. Preparation for church diversity includes specifying and affirming gender dynamics within the congregation. There is an increase in effective women leaders occupying senior level positions within organizations such as Fortune 500 companies, politics, government, military, and church denominations. Globally, more countries currently have a female president than at any other time in the history of the world. Discrimination against women based solely on their gender is nonsensical, especially within Christian communities that claim or profess to support female leadership at the highest levels of their religious organization. According to Judith Corbett Carter,

> Results showed that women used a collaborative leadership style and fostered a sense of community. As the research cited indicates, traits' impact on the way that women and men lead is inconclusive. However, in both secular and non-secular leadership style studies women exhibit more transformational leadership style qualities than men. More empirical evidence is necessary to validate the assumption that effective female and male clergy lead differently.[16]

To be sure, church diversity is more than race or culture. There are several other aspects and characteristics of personhood that help define and distinguish one person from another that cannot be explored in one book but should always be considered in all real-life contexts, such as class origin, education level, sexual orientation, and age.

The distance between academic scholarship and common everyday life has become wider. According to a prolific writer in the field of practical theology, Gerben Heitink, "Practical theology

16. Carter, "Gender Differences and Leadership Styles."

is related to intentional, more specifically, intermediary or me-
diative, actions, with a view to changing a given situation through
agogics."[17] Academic dialogue has too often been restricted to the
ivory towers of a few prestigious institutions and select communities. Information should not exist solely for individuals who possess diplomas, even as postsecondary education is almost essential
in today's society in order to live above the poverty line. A diploma
is no guarantee of knowledge, and a college graduate may be no
more intelligent than a person who has never set foot in a formal
academic institution. There is an unproductive type of elitism hov-
ering around various educational communities. Sadly, too many
Christians do not feel positively impacted by academia, along with
the irrelevancy of graduate theological education, and view church
life as insignificant.

As it pertains to church diversity, too many people content
themselves with a short cut, with what one might call an abbrevi-
ated version. Appropriate preparation allows a clergyperson and
a congregation to study multiple aspects of church diversity. In
most professions, if a person does not study her chosen profession
it is nearly impossible for her to be successful, or at least follow
the correct procedures. Few people are born experts, but the vast
majority of individuals improve through the process of learning.
It is essential for people (God's creation) to learn about God (the
Creator) through *study* and *reflection*.

Church diversity is a topic worthy of study; it can take an enormous amount of energy, commitment, and time, and usually entails
stretching our intellectual comfort zones. Often we are comfortable with the knowledge that we possess, but new knowledge has
the ability to threaten what we assume is legitimate. Studying has a
way of changing our original beliefs or thought patterns. Studying
requires asking questions, researching, and thinking in new ways.
Of course, some people do not possess the formal education to read
and comprehend some of the literature that exists; other people may
not possess certain skills needed for intense research. Nonetheless,

17. Heitink, *Practical Theology*, 8.

there are many who have more than enough education and skills, but who choose to walk blindly in ignorance.

More people should study church diversity, specifically cross-racial pastoral ministry and multicultural ministry. One reason religious communities are not doing well in church diversity is that few people are studying for pragmatic purposes. Studying helps people stay aware of what is going on instead of not having a grasp of current events. Show me a person who does not study and I will show you one who can be easily confused, frustrated, or lost in the specific subject area. Sad to say, there are many clergy and congregations who are confused, frustrated, or lost in the specific subject area of church diversity.

A lot of people say they have faith, but unfortunately they may not know much about the faith they practice. They may in turn possess little to no factual knowledge about their religion and denomination as it relates to church diversity. The word *faith* is commonly used in an attempt to hide one's lack of study, but it seldom works; in fact, it makes a mockery of the word *faith*, which has been defined as "belief; trust; confidence; conviction in regard to religion; system of religious beliefs; strict adherence to duty and promises; word or honor pledged." Some people use "faith" as an excuse for not studying and so fail to form a deeper, closer relationship with God as it relates to church diversity. But how can you have a relationship with something or someone you do not know?

The importance of the word *study* for pragmatic purposes is shown several times in the Old and New Testaments.[18] Studying is not a new concept that was invented for the pursuit of degrees of higher learning. Studying was a way of survival before humans ever opened any books. They had to study the seasons of the year in order to plant and harvest food at the correct time. They had to study animals in order to properly hunt for food without getting harmed or killed in the process. They had to study their newborn babies in order to ensure a present and future life. They had to study food to learn what was poisonous and what was edible. They

18. Concerning the importance of study, see Ezra 7:9–11; John 5:38–40; 2 Tim 2:15.

had to study materials in order to know what to build for shelter in the coldest weather, as well as in scorching heat. Study has been practiced for centuries so that humanity might live at its best, and we should not want anything less for ourselves today. We need to learn and grow with and for God by studying church diversity. Let's not make the mistake of assuming or walking blindly in the darkness of ignorance. Let's walk in the light of knowledge. The Gospel of John speaks of a light: Jesus Christ. I invite you to get to know, through church diversity, the expansive love of Jesus Christ.

Studying church diversity not only helps put you in tune with God and God's creation, but it also helps put you more in tune with yourself. All of humanity was created in the likeness of God. The Gospel of Matthew reminds us that it is important to acknowledge our brothers and sisters as we acknowledge God. Jesus instructed his disciples to pray what we have come to know as the Lord's Prayer, the first word of which is "our."[19] Humans are more than just flesh and bones, but are also spiritual beings that have a unique connection to one another and to God. We are placed in this world to do more than just eat, drink, and be happy or sad. We are more than emotional beings and physical beings; we are ultimately spiritual beings. Every individual consists of a diversity of behaviors, thoughts, emotions, experiences, among other traits. Diversity is embedded in us and all around us.

A small and steadily growing body of literature explores church diversity. Yet there is not enough. Some Christians believe that church diversity is not very important, or is not important at all. In fact, some Christians, by totally ignoring Jesus' instructions to his disciples, interpret the Scriptures as not conveying recommendations or commandments for church diversity.[20] It is a gift to study how, when, and where congregations can advance in church diversity. Though every congregation may not achieve the same level of diversity, Christians should trust the Holy Spirit to guide them in progressive directions. Courageous Christians in the past helped create a more diverse church; now religious communities

19. Jesus teaches the disciples how to pray in Matt 6:9–13.
20. Jesus' instructions to his disciples can be found in Matt 28:19.

need new bold and courageous leaders to do likewise. In many ways, the world is becoming smaller by the minute. An increasing number of communities, schools, and neighborhoods are situated in multicultural settings. It is now time for religious communities to embrace the diversity that is, in many circumstances, surrounding them on every side.

CHAPTER SUMMARY

Preparation is important for clergy and churches working toward cross-racial pastoral ministry and/or multicultural ministry. Without a *clergyperson's preparation*, there is a higher probability of negative consequences related to pastoral naiveté, lack of pastoral vision, and pastoral incompetency, which can contribute to a tragic outcome for all parties involved. Most people in the U.S. interact with members of other cultures at school or at work, or at least have some exposure to them through television and other media. Without a *church's preparation*, there is the likelihood of opposition from the laity toward the incoming clergyperson, of an environment devoid of a spirit of collaboration, and of resistance to move forward in God's grace.

Preparation takes time. Ideally, preparation should begin three to six months in advance of a cross-racial pastoral ministry or multicultural ministry. Through prayer, dialogue, and workshops, among many other activities, members can help ensure that the process is continually guided by the power of God's Holy Spirit.

3

The Welcome Introduction

SCENARIO #1

THE CONGREGATION HAS BEEN in a state of anticipation for several months with the news of their incoming pastor. What made this pastoral transition more rousing is that they were going to receive their first pastor of a different ethnicity. This cross-racial pastoral ministry was going to be the first in the history of their church. Many members were excited about the new possibilities afforded by this pastoral transition and what this could mean not only for their congregation but also for their surrounding community. Other members were reluctantly supportive of this new chapter in the life of their congregation and skeptical of any success from this kind of pastoral tenure. They were not going to invest much energy, faith, hope, time, or resources in this particular endeavor. Still, they decided to remain within the congregation to witness what would happen with the incoming pastor. A few members were vocal about their direct opposition to this type of church diversity. They were adamant that they spoke not only for themselves, stating that they also represented other members who were unwilling to speak on this issue.

The time for the welcome introduction activities was getting closer with each passing day. At this point, the congregation was developing feelings about the pending cross-racial pastoral ministry.

Experience reminded most of them that they never unanimously liked or supported their previous pastors, who were of the same ethnicity as the majority of the congregation. Many members were of the mindset that pastors were one part of the church but did not constitute the entire church. Besides, several members had seen pastors come and go. Many of the members recalled how they were always the remnant that journeyed together through the years and with different pastors. Now the time was finally upon them and a date set for the official welcome introduction event with their incoming pastor. The church fellowship hall was more crowded than usual. Surprising to a few, a substantial number of church members who had not attended Sunday morning worship services were present to meet their new pastor. An impressive number of community members who attended other churches or did not attend church at all were also present to meet the incoming pastor. This welcome introduction event was The Event to attend. At this moment, the incoming pastor and the pastor's family were surrounded by their new faith community with greetings, handshakes, and hugs. There were also abundant comments and questions directed not only at the incoming pastor but also the pastor's family. Some were questions of innocent curiosity, while others were loaded with meanings or inferences of which even the questioner was not cognizant. After a few hours the first official welcome introduction event was over, but there would be more opportunities for the incoming pastor and the congregation to get to know one another as they journeyed on their spiritual road together.

Today, a welcome introduction between a clergyperson and a congregation has taken on increased importance. This chapter explores the significance of the welcome introduction between the clergyperson and the church community for cross-racial pastoral ministry. It is essential for both parties to realize how important it is to lay a solid foundation at the beginning through team-building activities and "get to know you" events so that negative stereotypes and unhelpful prejudices can start to be dispelled and managed by personal interactions. The welcome introduction events should take place within the first one to three months of the pastoral tenure.

The purpose of mentioning the dynamics at this point is to highlight that church members will most likely bring strong opinions, impressions, and uninformed ideas about their incoming pastor, without any substantial experience with, or extensive knowledge of, the clergyperson, especially within a cross-racial pastoral ministry. The clergyperson will bring her own set of biases to this newly formed relationship as well. The welcome introduction is critically important as a starting point to address negative preconceived notions, and it can be done in a variety of ways.

A substantial amount of research shows that most people form a fairly strong opinion, impression, or idea of a person in a very short time—less than sixty seconds after meeting him or her. People also form opinions about others based on what they glean from television, books, newspapers, movies, songs, and other types of communication and entertainment. Belief systems about persons who are different may also be passed from one generation to another generation through family customs and traditions. Last but not least, personal experience can help create a perspective about people from other cultures.

Introductions usually set the tone for a variety of relationships, including the ones in the church. Various cultures ought to feel more comfortable meeting one another in religious settings than in secular environments. Since all people are ultimately God's creation, interaction in religious communities should have a feeling of "welcome home," and cultural differences can lead to healthy conversations. We can spend energy and time on our differences respectfully. During the welcome introduction, it can be acknowledged how church diversity enhances congregational life. It is useful to share visions of church diversity. Unrealistic expectations about church diversity during the welcome introduction are not productive. Kevin D. Dougherty observes that "neither congregations nor parishes are remotely close to approximating the diversity of the wider society and there are numerous questions regarding whether or not they should. Yet the concern expressed by faith groups about integration makes this an issue of continued importance."[1]

It is more beneficial to give an authentic and personal account of church diversity rather than a warm and fuzzy story that is totally irrelevant to the budding sacred endeavor in the religious community. It is not necessary to make grand declarations, but it is good to profess levels of commitment. As people of God, it is relevant in the beginning of any relationship to confirm solidarity as brothers and sisters in the oneness of Jesus Christ. Honesty is a key ingredient during the welcome introduction.

Currently, for a variety of reasons, a growing number of people across the United States, including church members, have a lower level of respect and a higher level of suspicion toward clergy. The pastoral role does not inspire the same honor or reverence as it did in the past. A few reasons for unfavorable pastoral perceptions include declining church attendance, increasing biblical illiteracy, instances of clergy criminality, and occurrences of congregational turmoil. We have generations of people who do not have a clear idea of the role of clergy and/or congregations. I have encountered these types of people during visits to worship services on Sunday, as well as some who have been members of my congregation. There needs to be more clarification and information on all levels within church life. A good time to convey important messages is during the welcome introduction process; however, it is not an appropriate time to have controversial debates or to make disparaging remarks about the faith community. To be sure, airing respectful disagreements is essential for the congregation, but there are other times for those types of discussions. Some people may be tempted to advocate for their preferred worship style (e.g., traditional or contemporary); others may be tempted to advocate for their preferred preaching style. Nevertheless, welcome introductions should primarily focus on *welcoming*.

There are a few ground rules that should be implemented during the welcome introduction process and practiced throughout the new clergyperson's tenure. Former pastor and current

1. Dougherty, "How Monochromatic Is Church Membership?"

public theologian Brian McLaren recommends the following "Ten Commandments"[2] to a congregation welcoming an incoming pastor:

I. Thou shalt not compare the old Pastor and the new Pastor, for the Lord thy God has made each person unique and wishes you to appreciate each original creation.

II. Thou shalt not expect everything to stay the same when the new Pastor arrives. Nor shalt thou resist change, nor assume that change is bad, but thou shalt trust that the Lord thy God isn't finished with your church yet and is bringing change for your good and the good of your mission.

III. Thou shalt not make graven images of thine old grudges, nor shalt thou keep stale disappointments in the temple of thine heart, but thou shalt forgive and move on in the grace of the Lord thy God, for how can thou ask God for mercy unless thou give mercy from thine heart?

IV. Thou shalt not commit gossip, nor shalt thou fearfully complain, nor shalt thou listen to those who do, but instead thou shalt entreat them to adjust their attitudes and lighten up, for everything shall be alright, and in fact, shall turn out very well indeed—better than you can even imagine.

V. Thou shalt not commit nostalgia or say that the old days were better, for in so doing thou shalt make thy judgment come true. Be assured that the Lord thy God is not falling asleep at the wheel, but will be with thee and surprise thee with abundant blessings, more than thou canst contain or count.

VI. Thou shalt not factionalize nor create "us-them" divisions, but thou shalt unify with thy brothers and sisters even when they annoy or confuse you.

VII. Thou shalt not come to the new pastor with your demands, pressure, complaints, bad reports, manipulations, threats, agendas, unsolicited advice, or snide comments. But thou

2. See http://www.brianmclaren.net/emc/archives/imported/ten-commandments-for-welcoming-a.html. Used by permission.

shalt say, "Welcome! How can we help you? We love you! We would like to increase our giving significantly. We're praying for you and your family. Welcome to our community! We baked you some cookies!" And each week, thou shalt do so again and again until the new pastor begs you to stop.

VIII. Thou shalt increase thy giving, and not withhold thy tithe, but invest thy money and thine heart in the future of thy community of faith and mission.

IX. Thou shalt not come to thine old and former pastor with anything but praise for the new pastor, but thou mayest bring thy concerns to God in humble prayer, and if thou must, thou may also share concerns with the duly appointed leaders of the church.

X. Most important, thou shalt trust God, and stay connected to God, and draw strength from God, staying deeply rooted in the message of God's grace. For God is good, and God will never leave you nor forsake you. You can count on that for sure!

I have personally experienced and observed how McLaren's "Ten Commandments for Welcoming a New Pastor" could have helped congregations with their incoming pastor. It amazes me how congregations can immediately insult or dismiss their incoming pastor at the welcome introduction, first introduction, or during the first year of being together. I am fairly sure that many members are unaware of their slights toward their incoming pastor. That is the principal reason for the value of McLaren's commandments. Congregations need to be educated about how to effectively welcome their incoming pastor.

Clergypersons, too, can make a lot of mistakes during the introductory phase that may contribute to the beginning of a combative relationship. Andy Rowell, assistant professor of ministry leadership at Bethel Seminary in St. Paul, Minnesota, offers the following "8 Pieces of Advice for a New Pastor":[3]

---

3. See http://www.andyrowell.net/andy_rowell/2008/06/7-pieces-of-advice-for-a-new-pastor.html. Used by permission.

1. Study the Scripture text you are going to preach on. Read two commentaries on the passage. If you and the commentators agree, you are on the right track. Preach it! Get this reference to help you find some good commentaries: *Commentary and Reference Survey: A Comprehensive Guide to Biblical and Theological Resources*,[4] by John Glynn.

2. Take walks just for the purpose of praying.

3. Learn everyone's name (first and last name) including the kids and janitor. Make your own photo directory or flash cards, if you need to.

4. Schedule as many meals and coffees with people as possible. Go to their workplaces and pick them up and take them to a place nearby that they often go to when they go out to lunch. These meetings should be forty-five minutes to an hour and a half—no longer. Pay and turn in the receipts to the church. But only order very basic (as opposed to extravagant) things at the restaurants—equivalent to the price of a burger and soda. No dessert or alcohol on the church's bill. I'm tempted to say on this one, "It is better to ask forgiveness than permission" because I think you should do it even if the church does not typically pay for these sort of things. You will not get fired for meeting with lots of people. It is difficult to do it if you don't meet at restaurants and coffee shops in this day and age. People don't have time to go to your house and people often don't host people in their homes. Every day meet with someone. Please! This is crucial.

There is a book called *Never Eat Alone and Other Secrets to Success: One Relationship at a Time*,[5] by Keith Ferrazzi and Tahl Raz. It is a good motto.

Questions to ask when you meet with people:

a. Where did you grow up? Where are all the places you've lived?

4. 10th ed. Grand Rapids: Kregel Academic, 2007.
5. New York: Currency Doubleday, 2005.

    b. What is your job? Can you tell me enough about it so I really understand what you do? Is it terrible or great or just so-so? Why? How is your relationship with your boss?

    c. What is your church background? Why did you come to our church?

    d. Should I just lift up these things we have already talked about to the Lord or is there something else I can pray about as well? (In other words, you will know enough already to be able to pray for them.) Do a quick prayer for them.

People will be surprised at how pleasant and interesting and good it is to meet the pastor, and you will be relieved not to get into all the church politics until you get to know people. This person is more important than their complaint about the church. When you get to know people, you will understand where they are coming from. The person who is passionate about missions grew up in Africa. The person who is passionate about pastoral care works in a nursing home. They are passionate for legitimate reasons!

As you can see from my questions, I would urge you to have low expectations for those first one-on-one meetings. The point is to get to know people. You will get close to some of them eventually. You will need to have difficult conversations with some of them eventually. But at this point, just enjoy people and get to know the basics. This is critically important to eventually ministering deeply to them.

Pastoring is one-third preaching (study, prep, reading), one-third administration (meetings, email, phone calls, mail, chaos), and one-third pastoral care (meeting with people). But you will have to initiate and be intentional to meet with anyone. Very few will reach out to you.

5. Read books by pastors for some sympathy. Read Eugene Peterson's books *The Contemplative Pastor*[6] and *Under the*

---

6. Grand Rapids: Eerdmans, 1993.

Unpredictable Plant.[7] Just read the stories if you get bogged down. Ditto David Hansen's *The Art of Pastoring.*[8] I would also recommend the Mitford books (fiction) by Jan Karon to get a sense of [the] warm personal pastoral ministry practiced by Pastor Tim.

6. Eventually, read some leadership books to help you analyze the organization. "Pastors overestimate what they can accomplish in one year and underestimate what they can accomplish in five years" (Sandy Millar, former vicar at Holy Trinity Brompton, London, England). Next year, when you get madly frustrated by the dysfunction of the organization of the church, you can read leadership books like *The Five Dysfunctions of a Team,*[9] by Patrick Lencioni, and his book *Death by Meeting;*[10] *Good to Great,*[11] by Jim Collins; *Primal Leadership,*[12] by Daniel Goleman; *First, Break all the Rules,*[13] by Marcus Buckingham [and Curt Coffman]; *Seven Practices of Effective Ministry,*[14] by Andy Stanley [et al.]; *Simple Church,*[15] by Thom Rainer [and Eric Geiger]; and *The Effective Executive: The Definitive Guide to Getting the Right Things Done,*[16] by Peter Drucker. In addition to these books, the article (available online for free) titled "How to Minister Effectively in Family, Pastoral, Program, and Corporate Sized Churches,"[17] by Roy M. Oswald, former Senior Consultant,

7. Grand Rapids: Eerdmans, 1992.
8. Downers Grove, IL: InterVarsity, 1994.
9. San Francisco: Jossey-Bass, 2002.
10. San Francisco: Jossey-Bass, 2004.
11. New York: HarperBusiness, 2001.
12. Boston: Harvard Business School Press, 2002.
13. New York: Simon & Schuster, 1999.
14. Sisters, OR: Multnomah, 2004.
15. Nashville: Broadman, 2006.
16. New York: Collins, 2006.
17. See http://bishopperryinstitute.org.au/uploads/Article%20~%20Church%20size%20and%20effective%20ministry%20%5BRoy%20Oswald%5D.pdf.

Alban Institute, was helpful for me. At a minimum, these books will help you realize that dysfunction in churches and other organizations is the norm but that there are some things you can do to start positive movement in the right direction. Will Willimon reports in his post "Non-synoptic Church Leadership in Church"[18] that he was given the following advice as a young pastor, which he now shares with others:

"I am sure someone has told you that you shouldn't change anything when you go to a new church for at least a year," an older, more experienced pastor said to me. Indeed, someone had told me just that. "Well, forget it! Don't change anything in a new church *unless you become convinced that it needs changing*! Change anything you think that needs changing and anything you think you can change without the laity killing you. Lots of churches are filled with laity who are languishing there, desperate for a pastor to go ahead and change something for the better. Lots of times we pastors blame our cowardice, or our lack of vision, on the laity, saying that we want to change something, but we can't because of the laity. We ought to just go ahead and change something and then see what the consequences are."

7. Get eight hours of sleep. Get to bed the same time every night and get up the same time. You will thus have more resources of patience to keep your cool as you encounter all kinds of craziness, dysfunction, and beauty. The sleep will help you from getting too discouraged. Expect the organization to be terrible! Expect the people to be great . . . once you get to know them.

8. Learn the history of the church. You need to be able to tell the old, old stories as well as anyone.

The welcome introduction phase is not the time for clergy to make pastoral declarations about the major changes they

18. See http://willimon.blogspot.com/2008/05/non-synoptic-church-leadership-in.html.

plan to make during their tenure. The incoming pastor will have plenty of meetings to elaborate on her plans in conjunction with the lay leadership. Incoming pastors have responsibilities toward their new congregation during the welcome introduction, and Rowell's "8 Pieces of Advice" can help the process tremendously. It is not enough for clergy to simply think everything good will happen on its own.

Two-way communication is a key factor for success during the welcome introduction phase. There should be dedicated time for a dialogue rather than solely a monologue. Good monologues may be an important part of welcome introductions, but pastors do not get enough time to listen to parishioners. Generally, parishioners do not get enough time to ask questions of pastors. The usual method of operation of church life primarily has parishioners listening to pastors. It is necessary to be aware that during the welcome introduction only limited information can be gathered. A first impression may be memorable, but at the most, it can only give a few clues and a few hints about a person. On more than one occasion, I have been informed by church members that *they knew all they needed to know* about their incoming pastor from the welcome introduction. In some instances, the information they received (or *perceived*) convinced them to remain active in the congregation. On other occasions, I have been informed by church members that *they knew everything* about their incoming pastor from the welcome introduction. In other instances, the information they received (or *perceived*) convinced them to distance themselves from the congregation or withdraw their membership. It should take more than an introductory meeting for any parishioner to make a decision regarding the incoming pastor. Similarly, it should take more than an introductory meeting for a pastor to make a decision regarding her new congregation. As in most relationships, communication during the welcome introduction can only convey a limited amount of information.

People look for different things regarding their new pastor during the welcome introduction. Some parishioners have great interest in knowing the incoming pastor's favorite TV shows, sports team, hobbies, and a host of other preferences. Other parishioners have a substantial amount of interest in their new pastor's level of education, type of education, and personal or professional life experiences. Geography tends to be a bonding opportunity, such as urban or rural, East Coast or West Coast, etc. If applicable, the new pastor's family will surely be thoroughly scrutinized and questioned by the new congregation. It is smart for the pastor and pastor's family to not seem indifferent or annoyed by the inquisition. The pastor and the pastor's family should always keep in mind that since they are entering a cross-racial pastoral ministry, people will most likely be more curious and eager to get to know them.

Let us not forget that the welcome introduction will only be the first phase of opportunity for the pastor and the parishioners to get to know one another. Therefore, they should not feel a need to cover everything all at once. The new pastor and the congregation should keep in mind that there will be numerous occasions for spending time together in Bible study, Sunday school, church meetings, retreats, and worship services, among other activities. The new pastor and her family should not feel the need to share their entire story. Too much information is usually not good to share, especially during the welcome introduction phase.

It is always good to lift up the name of Jesus Christ to help set the tone for the welcome event and to avoid focusing exclusively on the new pastor or the congregation. I believe that Jesus Christ is the most important component of any pastoral transition and any congregation. If a pastor is not careful, she may allow a congregation's size, affluence, location, and challenges (not to mention certain members) to overshadow Jesus. Likewise, if a congregation is not careful, issues pertaining to a pastor's family, popularity, or reputation may threaten to overshadow Jesus. Church folk have a habit of placing individuals on a pedestal or platform. It can be a long fall from grace. People of every culture too often flock to worship sports teams, pop culture idols, and even preachers of the gospel instead of Jesus Christ. We find people running to attend or participate in concerts and athletic events; what we really need is people running to lift up the name of Jesus Christ in the midst of church life at the very beginning of any relationship, including the welcome introduction.

Going back to the importance of good, two-way communication, let's remember that words are powerful! The old saying "Sticks and stones may break my bones, but words can never hurt me" is not totally true; words *can* hurt. But they also can heal as Christians live by, for, and on God's word. God's word ought to be conveyed during the welcome introduction through such means as song, reading of Scripture, and prayer. During any efforts toward greater church diversity, especially in the form of cross-racial pastoral ministries and increased multicultural activities, there is a lot of room for much-needed words of encouragement, inspiration, and instruction.

Hospitality is a holy action.[19] Churches have several official ceremonies and unofficial activities that display hospitality throughout the various stages of religious life. Welcoming is one form of hospitality that is an important church activity. Many congregations welcome newborn babies with ceremonies such as dedications or baptisms. Churches also welcome teenagers into their spiritual formation through confirmation and summer or winter vacation bible school. Churches welcome people for an entire lifetime—baptisms, confirmations, fellowship, etc.—and, in truth, they welcome people beyond death through funeral services and other associated activities. Churches welcome people into the life of their particular congregation, but ultimately, and more importantly, they welcome people into the Christian faith.

Entering into the Christian faith should be life-changing— forever. It should change the way you see yourself, other people, and the world. Cross-racial pastoral ministry and multicultural ministry call for a daily acknowledgment and acceptance of the other. Faithfully speaking, churches should make all people feel as though they belong. Churches should not make anyone feel unwelcome, unvalued, or unwanted. Cross-racial pastoral ministry and multicultural ministry require the people of God to exercise

19. A few examples of hospitality in the Scriptures: Rom 12:12–14; 1 Tim 5:9–11; Heb 13:1–3; 1 Pet 4:8–19; 3 John 1:7–9.

PRACTICAL THEOLOGY FOR CHURCH DIVERSITY

their Christian faith in spirit and *in truth* in practical ways associated with God's demands of cultural inclusivity. Churches are
responsible for welcoming their incoming pastor. It is noble when
churches welcome, for the first time, a new pastor who happens
to be of a different ethnicity, whether African-American, Asian-
American, Caucasian-American, or Hispanic-American. Brian
Bantum speaks in plain yet poignant terms on the topic of personhood within the Christian faith: "Being reborn in baptismal
waters, entering the world out of Christ's womb is being present in
the world in a new way. Being people of flesh and Spirit, mulattic
Christian existence disrupts through its presence and its demands.
These bodies of flesh and Spirit do not exhibit the physical de-
marcations of racial logic, but defy them through their union with
bodies of difference among them."[20]

During the welcoming process, it is important for the congregation not to overemphasize the fact they are welcoming a pastor of another ethnicity; rather, they should focus upon their new
pastor *as a person*. In the midst of cross-racial pastoral ministry
and multicultural ministry, the clergyperson's and the congregation's overarching messages to each other and to the world should
convey solidarity and kinship for the purpose of reflecting God's
kingdom and obeying God's commands. Of course, there are different gifts within the body of Jesus Christ. During the welcoming
process, however, it is paramount to focus upon unity as brothers
and sisters of one family, as children of God.

The welcome introduction process can be exhausting for both
pastor and congregation. The new pastor and the congregation
ought to remember that energy and intentionality will be useful
during the welcome introduction stage. They should remember,
too, that ministry is a partnership between very human beings.
Will Willimon writes, "Ministry is an intensely *human activity*.
The pastor is a 'parson'—literally, a 'person'—who works with individuals cooperatively in the parish. The pastoral ministry is an
activity. . . . The pastoral ministry cannot be done alone; it is a

20. Bantum, *Redeeming Mulatto*, 165.

cooperative human endeavor with an intense amount of human interaction. The pastorate is *socially established*."[21]

Willimon correctly highlights pastoring as a social enterprise between (but not exclusively between) the pastor and congregation. Cross-racial pastoral ministry and multicultural ministry endeavors cannot achieve success alone or unaided. The welcome introduction process is an ideal time to establish this joint partnership between the pastor and the congregation with great intentionality.

I learned that the first year is crucial for an incoming pastor to bond with a church community. I always try to talk to as many church members within the first seven months of a new pastoral ministry to establish an early pastoral rapport. My experience has taught me on many occasions that relationships matter, especially in church communities where time is essential. Pastors, like many leaders, are judged so quickly that most people believe they already know what leadership qualities will be displayed even before the clergyperson has served for a considerable amount of time.

WELCOMING STRATEGIES

One strategy of a welcome introduction for an incoming clergyperson to a cross-racial pastoral ministry is to have a meet-and-greet. The host can serve coffee, tea, and refreshments. The event (lasting from one to two hours) can take place at the home of one of the church members, a popular local gathering spot such as a restaurant, or the pastor's home if a number of church members help with set-up and clean-up. Home settings are preferred because they are more personal and intimate. It would be productive for people to introduce themselves to the incoming pastor and briefly describe their relationship with the church. If the clergyperson has family members present, it is important to engage them in conversation as well, since family members are greatly impacted by the new transition. The pastor's spouse, children, and other relatives

21. Willimon, *Pastor*, 308.

have to adjust, just like the new pastor. The family can also have great influence; in many situations, the success of a pastor's tenure largely depends on how well her family members transition into the faith community. When family members are present, all parties involved should remember the new pastor is not the only person in need of hospitality, instructions, and assistance.

The church and the incoming clergyperson are responsible for welcoming one another into their lives. The church bears responsibility because it has greater access to and familiarity with people and places in the community, as well as resources. It is the clergyperson's responsibility to allow the congregation to get to know her in appropriate ways. The church and incoming clergyperson give verbal and nonverbal signs indicating how closely they intend to walk with one another on their joint spiritual journey. The success of the relationship depends largely on a good beginning. Both parties need to be sensitive to the significant and long-lasting impact of the introduction phase, which is aptly called the *welcome introduction.*

One option is to have a series of welcome introduction events at various church members' homes. This option has multiple benefits—for example, a relaxed setting and the chance to invite neighbors—and it also makes available the opportunity for the incoming pastor to learn the demographics of the church members and surrounding community more rapidly. The climate of welcoming introductions should be deliberately hospitable.

Climate has to do with the general sense of warmth and good feeling members have toward each other. It also has to do with your congregation being a friendly, welcoming place for outsiders. Any congregation can benefit from building closer networks of relationships within the congregation.[22]

There will be plenty of opportunity during various church meetings, counseling ministry, and visitations for the incoming pastor to learn about any difficult circumstances, dysfunctional situations, or unhealthy relationships in the life of the church.

22. Oswald and Friedrich, *Discerning Your Congregation's Future,* 14.

Obviously, the welcome introduction phase is not the time to share that information.

SUGGESTED FORMAT FOR THE WELCOME INTRODUCTION EVENT *AT SOMEONE'S HOME*

Church members should feel free to host welcome introduction events at their homes. The invitation sends a message of support to the incoming pastor and the congregation. Church members should be mindful, however, that this is primarily a meet-and-greet occasion, and they should not impose their personal agenda during the gathering. I have been blessed with more than a decade of full-time pastoral experience, gained at four churches that span the East Coast, Midwest, and West Coast, and looking back I realize that those parishioners who invited me into their homes, visited my home, or hosted church events at their homes were almost always more committed than others to my pastoral tenure for the sake of God's church. Novice pastors need to understand that there is a correlation between fellowship outside the church and fellowship inside the church among people of faith. Churches are sacred spaces, but increasingly I am convinced that meetings in people's homes help bring members closer and build relationships. Relationships matter. It is good to utilize one's denominational resources or other appropriate material during the welcome introduction process at church members' homes or in the first few Sunday worship services.

The following is a suggested format for the welcome introduction event; those present may stand or sit in a circle:

- 1–2 minutes: opening prayer and/or reading of Scripture;
- 3–5 minutes: a self-introduction of the incoming pastor and the family members present;
- 5–10 minutes: a brief oral history by the incoming pastor of prior church ministry and pastoral experiences that prepared her for this new ministry;

- 2–5 minutes: an opportunity for each person to share his or her experience of the church or dreams for the church (optional);

- 2–3 minutes: closing words of gratitude; then encourage people to engage one another in conversation for the next 30–45 minutes;

- total time of event: 45–70 minutes.

Another strategy for a welcome introduction is to have an event at the church on a Saturday afternoon or Monday evening in the fellowship hall for two or three hours. This event should include attendance and participation by many of the committees within the church. It is appropriate to invite other churches, residents of the community, local businesses, and local civic organizations. This event can also have coffee, tea, and light snacks for a Saturday afternoon. A Monday evening event should include a light dinner. Again, if the clergyperson has family members present, it is important to engage them in conversation and also include them in the fabric of the welcoming process.

When a pastor is assigned to a group of people, it is a sacred occasion; it is also God's business. Spiritually speaking, through a variety of procedures, pastors can be sent to congregations for divine purposes. It is fine to mention the significance of the cross-racial pastoral ministry or multicultural ministry as it relates to a move forward in reflecting all God's creation. It is best to couch progress in church diversity in biblical terms to help keep the occasion holy and sacred. Shawchuck and Heuser write, "The multicultural congregation is to be desired and not feared. Revelation 5:9–10 makes no pretense concerning God's intention for the future of the worshiping community and for all humanity. From the perspective of the eschaton (the future age), the multi-cultural community is reconciled."[23]

23. Shawchuck and Heuser, *Leading the Congregation*, 238.

SUGGESTED FORMAT FOR THE WELCOME INTRODUCTION EVENT *AT CHURCH*

The following can take place while people are standing up or sitting in a circle:

- 1–2 minutes: opening prayer and/or reading of Scripture;

- 3–5 minutes: a self-introduction of the incoming pastor and the family members present;

- 5–10 minutes: a brief oral history by the church historian;

- 2–5 minutes: an opportunity for each person to share his or her experience of the church or dreams for the church (optional);

- 2–3 minutes: closing words of gratitude; then encourage people to engage one another in conversation for the next 30–45 minutes;

- total time of event: 45–70 minutes

A READING LIST FOR WELCOMING INTRODUCTION EVENTS AT CHURCH

- *Beginning Ministry Together: The Alban Handbook for Clergy Transitions*, by Roy M. Oswald et al. Bethesda, MD: Alban Institute, 2003.

- *The Welcoming Congregation: Roots and Fruits of Christian Hospitality*, by Henry G. Brinton. Louisville: Westminster John Knox, 2012.

- *Making Room: Recovering Hospitality as a Christian Tradition*, by Christine D. Pohl. Grand Rapids: Eerdmans, 1999.

- *Living into Community: Cultivating Practices That Sustain Us*, by Christine D. Pohl. Grand Rapids: Eerdmans, 2011.

• *Welcome, Pastor: Building a Productive Pastor-Congregation Partnership in 40 Days*, by Fred Oaks. Grand Haven, MI: FaithWalk, 2005.

TERESA OF AVILA'S INSTRUCTIONS ON SPIRITUAL RELATIONSHIPS

A substantial number of people, particularly the younger generation, are classifying themselves as "spiritual but not religious." They view their relationship with God as personal, and therefore they feel no strong obligations or ties to any denomination or local church. In fact, there is a growing population within Christianity that feels uncomfortable, and may even detest, corporate worship within the context of a local church or denomination. Those who hold this insular notion think of the church as being made solely by humanity and usually believe it has become too sinister to effectively challenge or forgive sin. People do operate within the church, and at times they make mistakes and allow injustices while seeking to live in righteousness, holiness, and peace in the midst of a chaotic world. On the other hand, it may equally be said that God created the church and it belongs to God!

It is important not to forget that much of the Bible, from the Old Testament to the New Testament, emphasizes the significance of following, serving, worshiping, and praising God—as a people. People have always joined together to perform the work of God, with capable leaders guiding them—figures such as Moses, who brought the Hebrews safely across the Red Sea; Joshua, who shepherded them into the promised land; and the Apostle Paul, who wrote letters of encouragement and instruction to the newly formed churches.

The word *Christian*, or follower of Jesus Christ, first appears in the Bible in the New Testament book of Acts (11:26). Christians devote their lives to the goal of spiritual transformation so that they might live eternally with God in heaven. Preachers and priests give numerous sermons throughout the year, advising their parishioners how to transform themselves from a sinful creature into a spiritual bride of Christ. There are many personal testimonies that are freely given by Christians in all kinds of social settings. These sincere testimonies express deep convictions about the best strategy for one's faithful soul to experience a spiritual transformation. There is no simple answer to the complex question of how people accomplish this task.

Teresa of Avila (1515–82) does offer an answer, which can be found in her book *Interior Castle*. Though she lived in the mid-sixteenth century, her influence can still be felt today. A Spanish Carmelite nun and mystic, she has been commonly referred to as St. Teresa of Jesus. In 1555, Teresa had a spiritual conversion while praying near a statue of Jesus. Shortly after her conversion, she quickly introduced reforms into the Carmelite Order—reforms that are still observed today within the organization—and she wrote books that are still read today. In *Interior Castle*, St. Teresa's description of spiritual formation includes a series of steps that one's soul must go through as if it were a diamond castle consisting of many rooms. The Christian's goal is to reach the innermost chamber where total communion with God takes place. There are many different stages, challenges, and obstacles that confront the faithful soul. Teresa gives advice on how one should navigate the way through to the center or innermost chamber. She also informs the reader that only through total dependence on God and God's mercy can one get there. The innermost chamber implies that there are other, outside chambers an individual must go through first. The first step toward one's spiritual formation, Teresa suggests, is to get to know one's self. It is difficult to welcome other people without welcoming oneself. She believed that knowledge of self was very important, and it is often overlooked by the vast majority of people. In fact, when we consider the extent to which we neglect to increase in self-knowledge, we should be ashamed. "It should cause us no little shame, that, through our own fault, we do not understand ourselves, or know who we are. As to what good qualities [there] may be in our souls . . . those are things we seldom consider and so we trouble little about carefully preserving the soul's beauty. All our interest is centered in the rough setting of the diamond."[24]

Teresa pinpoints one particular reason why people are not concerned about knowledge of self—their attention is directed toward objects that affect their bodies instead of their souls. Our bodies are only with us for a short while and can become broken at any given moment. She notes that people invest too much in superficial items and give minimal attention to their significant souls.

Prayer was very important for Teresa, and she thought it was essential to a Christian's life. Prayer is one of the most sacred ways for humanity to communicate with God. Most Christians believe, and are taught at an early age, that prayer changes things. Teresa believed that through prayer a person could reach spiritual transformation. Christians should place the worries of their future in God's hands and trust that through God's guidance everything will work out. Teresa described the following memorable experience: "I was told by a very learned man that souls without prayer are like people whose bodies or limbs are paralysed: they possess feet and hands but they cannot control them."[25]

Teresa believed prayer gives life to one's body and soul. Prayer is the communicating process between humanity and God that is generated from the physical realm to the spiritual realm, and back down to the physical. She believed that prayer helps humanity stay on the right path to spiritual transformation and assists faithful souls in entering hospitable relationships with one another. She acknowledged that people are frequently encouraged to become preoccupied with worldly activities to such a degree that they literally forget to pray; she would advise that prayer be one of the top priorities for every Christian in their spiritual transformation.

It is good when clergy and congregation acknowledge the importance of God in the foundation of the new relationship between them. In order for faithful souls to experience spiritual transformation, and progress closer to their innermost chamber, they must realize that they cannot do anything without God. With

24. Teresa of Avila, *Interior Castle*, 29.
25. Ibid., 31.

the acknowledgment of Christians' dependence on God they must also realize their weaknesses without the Creator. Teresa notes that Christians should "place their trust, not in themselves, but in the mercy of God, and they will see how His Majesty can lead them on from one group of Mansions to another and set them on safe ground."[26]

Faithful souls should not think that they are able to enter different stages of belief by their own ability. Teresa believed that a Christian should remain humble before her mighty God, implying that there is no other logical way for a Christian to act. Balancing good and evil is a constant struggle for all of humanity. Teresa believed this should promote a Christian's striving for spiritual transformation and the realization of the righteousness of God. Although humanity is plagued by faults and failures, she had total confidence that God was and is able to transform Christians into something more and allow them to experience communion with God. Spiritual transformation takes place when Christians understand that their souls are priceless; they have to protect their priceless souls and approach God with great humility. Christians must depend solely on God; only then will they enter into a faith that will lead them into communion with God.

CHAPTER SUMMARY

It is important to keep in mind that the welcome introduction event is an opportunity for the clergyperson and the congregation to become acquainted with one another. This is not a time for the clergyperson to be interviewed or interrogated, but a time for the congregation to convey their anticipation, excitement, and hope for new beginnings. This is not a time for the incoming pastor to make pastoral declarations about what is or is not going to happen during her pastoral tenure. Instead, the purpose of this event is for all parties to share who they are, rather than what they plan to accomplish. There is an old adage that goes, "People do not

26. Teresa of Avila, *Interior Castle*, 31.

care how much you know, until they know how much you care." The welcome introduction event is an ideal time for all parties to convey how much they care about church diversity in the form of cross-racial pastoral ministry by showing genuine hospitality from the beginning.

4

Collaborations

SCENARIO #1

ONE DAY I WAS attending a meeting of community leaders in South Carolina and a colleague at our table shared an interesting story with me related to his church life. Daniel Unumb, the executive director of Autism Legal Resource Center, informed me how his family recently hosted a visitor from Central Asia. Daniel's family proudly took their visitor to Sunday morning worship service at their church, to stores for shopping, and toured their neighborhood. Daniel informed me how his family and he had had a delightful time, as had their guest. In the course of one of their conversations, their guest made a revelatory comment; the conversation went along these lines:

Daniel: We are so happy you are here visiting us from Central Asia and we hope you enjoyed yourself. Share with us how you feel about what you have experienced and seen with us in this part of the United States.

Guest: Everything is nice, but I have to admit my surprise at one thing. It seems as if everyone is Caucasian and there is not a lot of diversity. I was surprised that the entire congregation was Caucasian—or at least there was no visible ethnic diversity. I have not noticed any racial diversity in this residential neighborhood. The stores we entered to shop barely had any cultural diversity. Again, everything is nice, but I am surprised by the lack of diversity.

Daniel: Thanks for sharing! I will work on the diversity component. Maybe it will get better by the next time you visit us. Thanks so much for being honest.

My associate Daniel began to describe how his guest's comments astonished him. He continued to explain, "My guest was correct— we are all white people in our congregation, the places we shop, the restaurants where we eat, and predominantly in our residential neighborhood. Ken, I am somewhat embarrassed it took someone from Central Asia to gently tell me I can use some more diversity in my life on a more intimate basis. What do you think, Ken? You are the pastor in our group!"

I gave the following multilayered response to Daniel:

First of all, Daniel, you have been a wonderful host to your guest from Central Asia. That was evident by inviting him into your home and taking him around the city to show him your authentic everyday life. Second, your guest most likely felt comfortable around you in order for him to share his candid thoughts with you. Third, many foreigners are surprised when they visit the U.S., which is one of the most diverse countries in the world. They have the impression that most of the different cultures engage one another by participating in shared activities on a daily basis. They are surprised to realize that much of the U.S. is divided along racial lines in many of our schools, our residential neighborhoods, and our religious communities. I think a good question to ask ourselves and explore has to do with the reasons we expect and often demand a certain type of racial or cultural diversity in many of our public spheres, such as police departments or hospitals and other valuable organizations, but we do not expect or demand the same kind of diversity in our congregations. Many religious organizations have much room for improvement in the area of church diversity. One of the ways this can be improved is by collaborations on multidimensional levels.

This chapter describes how various collaborations can occur with intentionality and thoughtfulness. Churches that intend to become increasingly diverse should adapt methods of operation with deliberate ways to work in partnership across ethnic boundaries for the glory of God in service in the world. Collaborations should take a multifaceted approach that includes intra-church components, inter-church relations, and outreach in a strategic manner throughout the year.

It would be foolish for pastors or churches to think that they can successfully navigate cross-racial pastoral ministry or any other major diversity pursuit without support from their neighbors. That is not to imply that all neighbors will be encouraging and will share the same vision of the church's inclusiveness. Some neighbors will be happier than others about a church's increased diversity. Some will be displeased, unhappy, and noticeably unhelpful; others, however, will want to help you in your efforts. You will want to quickly identify and warmly welcome those helpful neighbors in order to build bridges in a timely manner, because storms may arise. Unfortunately, in most cases, church neighboring has a lot of room for improvement, though we are called to be good neighbors to one another.[1]

INTRA-CHURCH COLLABORATION

When various church committees, groups, and leaders within the same faith community partner to work toward a specific goal, it is important for them to work with the pastor in the midst of a cross-racial pastoral ministry, because much of the laity will take verbal and nonverbal cues about the pastor from them. Church committees and leaders within any church setting can generate a great deal of havoc. There are many instances of pastors representing several faith traditions who fault certain church committees or church leaders for the demise of their pastoral leadership or pastoral tenure. Conversely, church committees and church leaders

1. See Exod 20:15–17; Prov 3:28–30; Mark 12:32–34.

also may have some legitimate concerns regarding their pastor's leadership. Nevertheless, pastors, church committees, and church leaders need one another in order for their faith community to operate most efficiently. When working harmoniously, they help construct a great deal of order in the context of a cross-racial pastoral ministry. The church committees and leaders can help relay encouraging messages to the rest of the laity; in turn, the entire laity can help relay optimistic messages to the local community. Then, before too long, the world will know the good news of the love of Jesus Christ's disciples forming church communities regardless of race. This requires patience, because as you may already know, bad news usually travels faster than good news.

It is always good for the pastor to have support from a broad spectrum of the congregation, especially in cross-racial ministry. Intra-church collaborations help keep the pastor from working (or being perceived as working) only with particular groups within the church. The appearance of non-collegiality can lead to an atmosphere of church division along racial lines. The pastor and the congregation may be perceived as unwilling to work with each other due to their differences, with race being the easiest identifier or indicator, regardless of the accuracy. It is essential for the pastor and congregation to realize it will take a *deeper* level of commitment (or at least a *different* level of commitment) to support cross-racial ministry and other church diversity efforts.

Intra-church collaboration is valuable because it allows less room for detractors of church diversity and helps reduce mistakes and misunderstandings. One way to ensure successful collaboration in advancing church diversity is through strategic communication between vested persons. Two church consultants, Roy M. Oswald and Robert E. Friedrich Jr., illustrate an excellent approach for intra-church collaborations: "Fundamentally they must be committed parishioners who understand the process and are willing to work. Ideally, they should represent a cross section of the congregation, with some relative newcomers, some old-timers, people with a variety of theological perspectives, and a balance of genders and any other factors that are significant in your congregation."[2]

Oswald and Friedrich are correct in identifying committed parishioners as fundamental to the success of church diversity. In truth, committed parishioners can help make the most incompetent pastor an effective clergyperson. Those particular pastor-parishioner joint ventures have been going on for millennia. For collaborations to be most effective, it is imperative for various groups within the church to be able to voice their joys, concerns, challenges, and dreams concerning church diversity in a safe space.

Church collaborations are important in a world quickly becoming a global village. It is increasingly difficult for church communities to exist or thrive with an insular mindset or an intolerant attitude. A few congregations, churches, national denominations, and other religious communities are intentionally attempting to become more multicultural in order to reflect God's creation. In order for them to become healthy and vibrant, however, the senior pastor must exhibit certain major characteristics to be effective.

One method of collaboration is through intercultural pastoral care and counseling. This includes the acknowledgment and appreciation of various cultures. In church diversity, it is essential for all people to feel significant. Most people have a primal need to feel loved, to know that they matter. Effective intercultural pastoral care and counseling does not overlook such traits of a person's body as age, gender, and ethnicity. Elizabeth Conde-Frazier writes, "Cultural majority congregations need to become aware of their own cultural imperialism by making a practice of affirming the cultural heritage of each person and by teaching attitudes of respect and appreciation toward other cultures. Respect is not demonstrated by becoming blind to cultural differences; this simply renders them invisible."[3]

Parishioners seek to worship God in spirit and in truth. People of various cultures who are members of a church should be able to celebrate who God created them to be in their respective

2. Oswald and Friedrich, *Discerning Your Congregation's Future*, 22.

3. Conde-Frazier, "Spiritual Journey toward Peaceful Living," 163

heritage. Effective intercultural pastoral care and counseling from the dominant culture will acknowledge and celebrate others, such as African-American and Native-American heritages, within their congregation. This acknowledgment and celebration may be displayed in various ways—through songs, prayers, preaching styles, pastoral care, and pastoral counseling that reflect and nurture the realities of a multicultural congregation. For racial minorities to have their racial identity ignored in worshiping God is often hurtful.

Another major characteristic of effective intercultural pastoral care and counseling is ensuring that power dynamics are balanced within multicultural ministry. Since power dynamics are typically controlled by the dominant economic-political culture, it is important to prevent one culture from having a monopoly in multicultural ministry. Eric Law writes, "Teaching a white group to bear the cross is totally appropriate in a multicultural setting."[4] Just as in secular multicultural settings, people's roles typically do not change within multicultural religious communities. For example, when racial segregation was in its prime in the secular community, it was in its prime within the religious community. African-Americans were relegated to sit in certain sections of Caucasian churches or totally segregated from their Caucasian counterparts, just as they were forced to live and work in certain neighborhoods. To quote Eric Law again, "Teaching people of color about bearing the cross first is not appropriate. That is like teaching poor persons that they have to sell all their possessions and give them to the poor. You do not have to choose the cross when you are already on the cross. Instead, we should be teaching blessedness, the empty tomb, the resurrection, and Easter celebration."[5]

Ministering justly to a multicultural congregation is difficult work. Congregations are typically looked upon as the reason why multicultural diversity attempts fail. Competent leadership in multicultural ministry demands brave leadership. Effective intercultural pastoral care and counseling will seek to empower the

4. Law, *Wolf Shall Dwell with the Lamb*, 56.
5. Ibid., 57.

powerless and disempower the powerful.[6] Pastoral care and counseling needs to be looked at more closely in multicultural ministry as a key factor.

Collaborations are not automatic or easy in most contexts, including religious communities. The power dynamic particularly resonates within specific ethnic groups, such as Native-Americans, who have been oppressed by religious communities. Native-Americans, like all people, should have the ability to express themselves freely. It is well documented that a great number of Native-Americans were brutally forced to accept Christianity or be killed at the hands of Caucasian Christians. There are stories of Native-Americans responding to the question of "Do you want to go to heaven?" with "No, if the white man or white oppressor is going to be there." This kind of history impacts all parties involved. Native-Americans need to feel that their ethnic identity is not taken away from them when they walk into a Caucasian church. Years ago, when I served in the Detroit Annual Conference of the United Methodist Church, I witnessed Native-Americans participating every year in the annual church conference worship services, with their native clothes, music, language, and pipe-smoking. As a transplant from the Southeast, unfamiliar with Native Americans, I asked a colleague sitting near me, "What is going on in here? Are we in church or a party?" My colleague responded, "They are worshiping God in spirit and in truth. They are being authentically themselves and not what we want them to be." I do believe Native-Americans want to go to heaven as much as any other people. But like any other people, they do not want to have to imitate another ethnicity to gain entry.

Western history books have traditionally ignored people of color or minimized their contributions to civilization. What effects does systematically being ignored have on a people? Edward P. Wimberly writes, "Caring within a local black congregation is a response pattern to God's unfolding story in its midst. This unfolding story is one of liberation as well as healing, sustaining, guiding, and reconciling. As a response to God's story, the caring resources

6. Ibid., 74.

of the local black church are used to draw those within the church, as well as those outside the church, into God's unfolding story. By being drawn into God's story, people find resources of care and love to meet their everyday needs."[7]

It is essential that all people's stories merge with God's story in an affirmative way. Congregations should provide healthy and wholesome religious teachings that provide positive reflections for people of all races.

In the context of church diversity, clergy and lay leaders should gather data about their parishioners and community. There are some noticeable differences within congregations that are predominantly African-American, Caucasian, or Native-American. It would be advantageous for church leaders to be familiar with the various similarities and differences in order to meet their needs. How does one obtain information for a multicultural ministry? Emmanuel Y. Lartey writes, "Healthy 'race relations' within any community must be based on knowledge and information about the groups constituting the community. The approach to the multicultural society favored here is that of 'facts and figures' as providing the necessary tools for effective action. As such, an attempt is made to build profiles of the various ethnic communities in the society which seek to give information about, for example, social customs, religious rites, food habits, leisure activities, family patterns, gender roles, education and housing within each group."[8]

Acquiring accurate information is essential for church diversity. Competent clergypersons and thoughtful lay leaders should know their congregation and do some research about the congregation's locale. Just as those in the military and diplomatic service must acquaint themselves with a country's culture before their arrival, clergy and laity engaged in church diversity should have knowledge of various cultures.

7. Wimberly, *African American Pastoral Care*, 24–25.
8. Lartey, *In Living Color*, 169.

SUGGESTED FORMAT FOR A MEETING FOR *INTRA*-CHURCH COLLABORATIONS

People may stand or sit in a circle during the following:

- 1–2 minutes: opening prayer and reading of Scripture by the new pastor or a church leader;

- 3–5 minutes: an opportunity for each chairperson to share her responsibilities or dreams for the church;

- 3–7 minutes: an opportunity for the new pastor to summarize what was said by the chairpersons and add some words of encouragement or insight;

- 10–20 minutes: an opportunity to respond to a series of questions on paper or through discussion:

  1. What are three to five goals we would like to accomplish?

  2. What are two or three strategies we can implement so that we accomplish our goals?

  3. How can we inform and excite the congregation so that it embraces our ideas?

  4. What are our one-month, three-month, seven-month, and nine-month milestones for progress?

  5. How are we through this activity following Jesus Christ and glorifying God?

Total time for meetings of this nature should be around forty-five minutes and no longer than ninety minutes. It is prudent to include specific goals or objectives for intra-church collaborative meetings to help keep people focused and engaged. Strategic meetings are necessary for church diversity to succeed. Many of the more efficient meetings I attend include a concise agenda with a few clear objectives and an outline of a plan of action. Effective meetings can help bring the most nascent idea to its full development and an eventual "mission accomplished." On the other hand, unproductive meetings can deflate the best idea or limit any chance of accomplishing anything. As Oswald and Friedrich note, research shows that bad meetings have serious repercussions: "At the top of Alban researchers' list of the things that contribute most to lay leader burnout is atrocious meetings. What we make people endure during the course of a meeting is often brutal. People labor for hours, go home exhausted and needing to go to work the next day, and wonder what that was all about."[9] To remain focused during these meetings it is useful to incorporate relevant Scripture and materials supporting church diversity endeavors. Meetings on the topic of church diversity should always be presented as a blessing and not a burden.

INTER-CHURCH COLLABORATION

When churches partner to work toward a specific goal, they can help create positive synergy for one another, learn from one another, and assist one another. It is easy for some to feel isolated in the midst of their church diversity efforts, because most churches have other priorities or pursue other objectives. Inter-church collaborations can provide prayerful support, fresh perspectives, and accommodating allies for the pastors and the laity. It is important for churches to partner with a diverse group of faith communities. Inter-church collaborations can occur cyclically, based upon the liturgical calendar, such as during Christmas, Lent, or Easter; they can also occur systematically, during activities such as athletic events, musical events, and outreach projects.

Inter-church collaborations exhibit unity between religious communities. Churches need to complement one another rather than compete with one another. A glaring (and shameful) hypocrisy may be evident to younger people when they observe primarily all-white, all-black, all-Hispanic, or all-Korean church gatherings, while hearing messages about God loving and accepting all people. How embarrassing for a congregation when people experience diverse fellowship in areas other than church life! The younger generations, who are generally accustomed to multicultural

9. Oswald and Friedrich, *Discerning Your Congregation's Future*, 11.

settings, tend to be more comfortable with church diversity. Unlike fifty years ago, young people now experience racially integrated schools, restaurants, professional sports events, concerts, and television shows. Younger people often feel disconnected when they experience the church's non-collaborative method of operating along racial lines. Consequently, many of them withdraw from church life.

Inter-church collaborations pertaining to church diversity should occur on both a pastoral and a congregational level. On a pastoral level, clergypersons are able to help God's word become more alive and relevant to their members and the larger community. Not surprisingly, as James Berkley writes, "one 'picture' of cross-cultural friendship exhibited by two leaders will be more effective than a thousand sermons."[10] Pastoral collaborations can occur by having a clergyperson of a different ethnicity serve as a guest preacher during worship or as a guest lecturer during retreats. On a congregational level, guest choirs from various cultures can be invited to sing, or an assortment of musicians from other traditions can perform, along with other invitations to diverse groups.

Churches should partner with organizations toward noble ventures locally, nationally, and internationally. It is useful for congregations to look, focus, and work outside their walls in creative ways with the community. This can be done by congregations partnering with different non-church groups such as Boy Scouts, Girl Scouts, homeless shelters, food banks, grade schools, and other organizations. Community partners can be helpful to congregations.

SUGGESTED FORMAT FOR A MEETING FOR *INTER*-CHURCH COLLABORATION

People may stand or sit in a circle during the following:

- 1–2 minutes: opening prayer or reading of Scripture by a pastor or layperson;

10. Berkley, *Leadership Handbook of Outreach and Care,* 189.

- 3–5 minutes: an opportunity for each church representative to share his or her dreams for the church partnership(s);

- 3–7 minutes: an opportunity for a pastor or layperson to summarize what was said by each church representative and add some words of encouragement or insight;

- 10–20 minutes: an opportunity to respond to a series of questions on paper or through discussion:

  1. What are one or two goals we would like to accomplish?

  2. What are two or three strategies we can implement to help us accomplish our goals?

  3. How can we inform and excite our churches so that they embrace our ideas?

  4. What are our one-month, three-month, seven-month, and nine-month plans for progress?

  5. How are we through this activity following Jesus Christ and glorifying God?

As previously noted, the total time for meetings of collaboration of this nature should be around forty-five minutes, and no longer than ninety minutes. It is prudent to include inter-church specific goals or objectives for *intra*-church collaborative meetings to help keep people focused and encouraged.

AN INCREASINGLY GLOBAL CHURCH

Citizens of the United States often take a lot of things for granted. Many Americans assume that certain privileges are God-given rights that should automatically be given to all of humanity. Younger generations of Americans usually have less experience or less knowledge of the racial and cultural struggles in the country's past. Visiting other countries has allowed me to see more clearly the dynamics of an increasingly global church. The church in the United States is one of the wealthiest faith communities in the world. American churches have relatively large budgets, own a good deal of property, often are associated with prestigious colleges and universities, and operate a multitude of institutions such as hospitals and retirement communities.

It seems as if the average person living in the U.S. has compassion for citizens of developing countries. This is especially evident as congregations sponsor mission trips to developing countries and provide financial aid for various projects there. Ironically, many of the same churches would be reluctant to receive people from the developing world into full membership. In order to embrace the reality of an increasingly global church, it is best to remember that Christianity is much more powerful than the United States. Christianity is older and larger than the U.S., and it stretches around the globe, across six continents, and reaches into the heavens. Sadly, too many Christians living in the U.S. relegate their faith to a nationalistic understanding, which may lead to the exclusion people of a different nationality or ethnicity.

A congregation's ability to incorporate a variety of cultures into its faith community is essential to its future in a world that has become a global village. Pastors and parishioners must have a sensitivity that goes beyond their own experiences, understandings, and comfort zones. A religious community's message and mission should convey *caring for all people* rather than *caring for our people*. If congregations refuse to fully integrate other ethnicities into the fabric of their faith community, they will eventually experience a loss of vitality and may even cease to exist. One reason for the closing of churches all across the U.S. every year is their inability or refusal to collaborate on any level with people of different cultures. Many clergy and congregations do not have sufficient resources to collaborate in an increasingly diverse world. The U.S. remains one of the most respected and prosperous countries, and people from all over the globe seek permanent residency here. This has led many American community organizations and institutions within the fields of education, health care, and law enforcement to provide training for their members in engaging foreigners. Pastors and parishioners need training and education for a broad understanding of religion and spirituality in order for church diversity to grow into a reality that lovingly embraces God's global village.

A READING LIST FOR CLERGY AND CONGREGATIONS ABOUT GOD'S GLOBAL VILLAGE

- *Ministering Cross-Culturally: An Incarnational Model for Personal Relationships*, by Sherwood G. Lingenfelter and Marvin K. Mayers. Grand Rapids: Baker Academic, 2003.
- *Cross-Cultural Servanthood: Serving the World in Christlike Humility*, by Duane Elmer. Downers Grove, IL: InterVarsity, 2006.
- *Cross-Cultural Connections: Stepping Out and Fitting in Around the World*, by Duane Elmer. Downers Grove, IL: InterVarsity, 2002.
- *Leading Cross-Culturally: Covenant Relationships for Effective Christian Leadership*, by Sherwood G. Lingenfelter. Grand Rapids: Baker Academic, 2008.
- *Half the Church: Recapturing God's Global Vision for Women*, by Carolyn Custis James. Grand Rapids: Zondervan, 2011.
- *Leading Across Cultures: Effective Ministry and Mission in the Global Church*, by Jim Plueddemann. Downers Grove, IL: InterVarsity, 2009.
- *Global Church Planting: Biblical Principles and Best Practices for Multiplication*, by Craig Ott and Gene Wilson. Grand Rapids: Baker Academic, 2011.
- *God's Global Mosaic: What We Can Learn from Christians around the World*, by Paul-Gordon Chandler. Downers Grove, IL: InterVarsity, 2000.

Since the United States is an extremely diverse country, one of the most diverse in the world, a noble goal is to have congregations play an important role in showing how various cultures can collaborate in a respectful manner. Clergy and congregations should have an honorable role in global competency. There is a need for more religious leaders willing to take leaps of faith in church diversity, which will have miraculous impacts within the United States.

Courageous leaders do not idly stand still and watch situations fall into disarray. Too many cultures in the U.S. are in conflict because of lack of communication, which is a key ingredient in effective collaboration. There are a few places in this country where certain types of church collaborations occur. However, religious communities are experiencing ample conflict on every level of their organizations, from the congregational level to the denominational level. There is a lack of religious leadership that addresses church diversity through collaborations. A growing number of younger Christians are grappling with being residents of one of the wealthiest countries in the world and belonging to some of the wealthiest Christian faith communities in the world, while witnessing other people from various ethnicities struggle with being excluded from God's church in the U.S.

Rather than a condemnation of the current status of church collaborations, this chapter is a critique in which there are great expectations, high hopes, and grand visions of new possibilities for clergy and congregations to improve on the present state of church diversity.

A READING LIST ABOUT VARIOUS CHURCH COLLABORATIONS

- "The African American Church and University Partnerships: Establishing Lasting Collaborations," by Rudolph S. Jackson and Bobbie Reddick. *Health Education & Behavior* 26 (1999) 663–74.

- "Addressing Health Needs of an Aging Society through Medical-Religious Partnerships: What Do Clergy and Laity

Think?" by W. D. Hale and R. G. Bennett. *The Gerontologist* 43 (2003) 925–30.

- "Church-State Partnerships: Some Reflections from Washington, D.C.," by Carol J. De Vita and Pho Palmer. *New York Times*, September 30, 2003.

- "Brooklyn Bishop Is Facing Diverse Cultures and Tensions," by Peter Steinfels. *New York Times*, February 22, 1990. http://www.nytimes.com/1990/02/22/nyregion/brooklyn-bishop-is-facing-diverse-cultures-and-tensions.html.

- "Community of Diversity, and Now, of Tragedy." *New York Times*, March 15, 2003. http://www.nytimes.com/2003/03/15/nyregion/community-of-diversity-and-now-of-tragedy.html.

- "Southern Baptists Approve Steps Aimed at Diversity," by Erik Eckholm. *New York Times*, June 15, 2011. http://www.nytimes.com/2011/06/16/us/16baptist.html?_r=0.

- "Crystal Cathedral May Lose Spanish-Language Ministry," by Nicole Santa Cruz. *Los Angeles Times*, November 19, 2011. http://articles.latimes.com/2011/nov/19/local/la-me-crystal-cathedral-20111119.

SCENARIO #2

A pastor is meeting with parishioners about a specific topic related to the possibility of collaborations. All of a sudden the discussion takes a variety of turns to highlight a multitude of reasons why collaborations may not work. Then quickly, the conversations go from reasons the collaborations may not work to reasons the collaborations cannot work. A few people in the meeting try to help lead the discussion toward possible solutions, but the tidal wave of negativity, pessimism, and hopeless attitudes is too forceful for optimism, confidence, and teamwork to prevail. The attendees of this meeting neglected to highlight some successful examples of church collaboration or other resources that could possibly assist them in reaching their goals. The tone in the room begins to feel like a combination of a tragic accident and a funeral ceremony. The idea of possible church collaboration endeavors is now impaired and dead on arrival. By the end of this meeting, most of the attendees have convinced themselves there is no need to expend any of their limited time, energy, and resources, because the collaborations simply will not work. They did succeed at what they have been doing too well for too long: talking themselves out of new and creative collaborations.

In my pastoral ministry, which spans more than a decade, I have personally experienced and observed a number of church meetings similar to the above scenario. A great many pastors and parishioners across the country have shared with me their reluctance to bring anything new regarding collaborations to church meetings, because of a lack of enthusiasm, receptiveness, and support. I have learned there is a skill in conducting productive church meetings. A lot of pastors and parishioners should feel ashamed, if not guilty, for wasting precious time in church meetings lamenting what they have not accomplished and cannot accomplish. During Sunday morning worship, millions of Christians in the U.S. sing, pray, and preach about all they can do through Jesus Christ. Then, Monday through Friday, millions of those same Christians give a laundry list of excuses for the kinds of Christian work they cannot accomplish. One of the quickest ways to lose a new visitor or new member is to have him or her attend a dysfunctional church meeting. This method of conducting church meetings is contributing to the closing of many congregations.

There are growing numbers of Christians who feel more connected to God in ways that do not involve becoming active in a congregation. Without a doubt, people are feeling connected to Jesus Christ in new ways, many of which do not include a church community. Rather, they are electing to turn to television, radio, and Internet ministries as well as other spiritual experiences. We have former traditional church folk who have fled local congregations without any intention of returning. We have younger generations who have no intention of sitting in a pew. Pastors and parishioners do not have the time to explore any kind of goodwill collaboration in the U.S., which is too often divided by class, gender, and race. Pastors and parishioners of every culture should be collaborating in creative and new ways with people of every generation, class, gender, nationality and race to help connect them to Jesus Christ's grace, love, and power.

RECOMMENDATIONS FOR *PRODUCTIVE* CHURCH MEETINGS ABOUT COLLABORATIONS

Biblical passages that support productive meetings include the following:

- Matt 5:13–16; 9:35–38; 18:1–9
- Mark 6:30–44; 9:33–37; 12:13–17
- Luke 5:1–11; 6:43–45; 15:1–7
- John 10:1–21; 13:1–17; 15:18–27
- 1 Thess 1:1–10; 3:6–13; 4:12–28

1. Write an agenda for the meeting and remain on the topic at hand.
2. Set a time limit for the meeting.
3. Invite a guest with experience in successful church collaborations to share one or two examples.
4. Bring in resources such as a newspaper or magazine article, book, or video about successful church collaborations.
5. Bring in the partner(s) for the potential church collaboration for discussion, and give most or all attendees a ministry related to the church collaboration endeavor.
6. Begin the meeting with prayer or read an applicable Scripture passage.
7. Invite everyone to ask a question or comment on the possible collaboration.

8. Create a plan-of-action list toward the conclusion of the meeting.

9. End the meeting with prayer.

Congregations are one of the few organizations that can be in a state of decline for decades and not progressively seek techniques for change. They will actually admit how long they have been in a state of decline without seriously exploring any new methods of collaboration. Many other organizations will be in a state of decline for several months to one year and then utilize all the resources within their reach in their efforts to move forward. They may admit their declining status, but they are also aggressively collaborating with partners in order to stimulate growth. If their efforts do not work, you will soon find a "Closed" sign on the door. Most organizations will not be in a constant state of decline and will continue to offer their services to a community. I am referring to organizations with a hundred times more financial resources than one congregation. Not one Fortune 500 company would allow one of their businesses to operate in a specific location if it were experiencing decades of decline. On the brighter side, millions of congregations across the country are gathering on a weekly basis with literally only a few faithful followers.

It is insulting that so few congregations have taken it upon themselves to be responsible for the common good of nations. Some organizations based in the U.S., such as the Bill & Melinda Gates Foundation, have taken it upon themselves to try to make a difference through the power of collaboration. It is good to see them using their wealth and influence for the good of all humanity, with special attention given to those who are different from the predominant culture. Where are the others like Bill and Melinda Gates? Christian congregations have been biblically mandated to help make this world a better place to live. Promoting peace, harmony, and justice starts with one person at a time and one congregation at a time.

5

Some Possible Challenges

SCENARIO #1

A MIXED CROWD FILLED the room: pastors, parishioners, men and women of various ethnicities, cultures, and nationalities. They had gathered together to explore options in the pursuit of increasing church diversity in their religious communities. Some of the parishioners did not have extensive experience in church life; however, they brimmed with an excitement that could be felt in the air. Some of the clergy were just beginning their careers. They had not been in pastoral ministry in the context of a local church for a long period of time. Most of the pastors and parishioners in attendance, despite having little church experience, believed they were going to change their congregation for the better in no more than five years and change their denomination in no more than ten years. They believed, rightly, that God loves everyone; but they wrongly believed that they inherently loved everybody, similar to the way God loves. Some of them had never experienced church conflict. Most of the pastors believed they would lead a congregation similar to the one they were raised in, with the same kind of people who genuinely liked them and supported them. They had good intentions and were not intimately aware of many of the pitfalls, battles, and demands of pastoral ministry in the context of pastoring a congregation. It would not take long for them to learn firsthand the tasks, tests, and trials of pastoral leadership.

Some of the clergy in attendance had not only witnessed but also experienced how the various storms within congregations could cause serious harm. Some parishioners in attendance had observed and endured insults or injuries within church life. Through it all, they were present in the room to explore more noble endeavors related to church diversity in the context of their congregation. Many congregants had been tempted to leave their church on several occasions but were unwilling to depart from their faith community; nearly all concluded a long time ago that not only did they need the congregation, but the congregation needed them to be constructive. Their commitment to the church helped lead them to this particular room with some like-minded people to learn, train, and strategize in order to further church diversity in their ministry.

Church leadership is a complex notion. Pastoral leaders and lay leaders should work together to bring healing, health, and wholeness to the congregation. There is not enough honest dialogue in congregational life. Congregations need to have more candid discussions about the complications. A growing number of Christian communities are facing the harsh reality that their members are not immune to hardships such as alcohol abuse or addiction, drug abuse or addiction, parent-child conflict, divorce, physical illness, anger, and a host of other challenges. When straightforward dialogue does not occur in appropriate ways, the possibility of miscommunication dramatically increases. Another result of remaining silent on urgent issues that negatively impact church folk is the likelihood that they will feel ostracized, isolated, or uninformed on how to navigate some of life's most difficult hurdles. People from all walks of life need to be encouraged and equipped when they join a congregation for spiritual nourishment. Howard Clinebell writes,

> In working with persons from different ethnic, cultural, or sexual backgrounds, it is essential to be aware of the universal tendency to feel, on some level, that one's own

experiences and culture are the norm for all human beings. Each of us judges cultural differences as inferior, according to the degree this tendency operates in us. It may
blind us to subtle but significant differences in the ways
counselees from other backgrounds perceive, conceptu-
alize, feel, solve problems, and create their world-view.[1]

There are widespread challenges to church diversity. History informs us that church members from several congregations in the
United States have racially discriminated against one another, refusing church membership, denying church leadership positions,
and engaging in other prejudicial practices. One manifestation of
this dishonorable legacy is how numerous Christian denominations are separated primarily along ethnic lines. Humans have a
tendency to criticize and condemn the unfamiliar, especially unfamiliar people. Neighborhoods, workplaces, and schools sometimes consist of people who are unfamiliar with one another. Some
challenges to church diversity are associated with cultural and territorial conflict, identity crisis, and a lack of resources.

Within a religious context, one challenge to cross-racial
pastoral ministry and multicultural ministry is a lack of resources
in the form of literature, education, and training. There is not an
adequate supply of books, magazines, and journals that critically
engage the topic of church diversity. Sadly, only a few writers in the
academy or in popular culture are interested enough to explore,
research, and publish findings on the need for improvement in
race relations in the church. As a result, congregations suffer in
not knowing pragmatically how to become interracially unified.
Furthermore, the graduate theological educational process does
not analytically engage the notion of church diversity in a practical manner. In the past twenty-five years, graduate theological
schools have had some difficulty employing professors with substantial pastoral experience to teach seminarians in preparation
to serve the church. Along the same lines, at present, the number
of seminary professors with any amount of pastoral experience in
cross-racial ministry and multicultural ministry is dismally small.

1. Clinebell, *Basic Types of Pastoral Care*, 101.

Again, as a consequence, congregations have a poor record when it comes to race relations, while other organizations succeed at a higher rate. There needs to be an abundance of literature in all aspects of church diversity that parallels other significant topics such as church history and church theology. In order for churches to make progress in race relations and, in many cases, continue to exist, they must learn to accept people of different ethnicities and praise and worship God together. Seeking greater diversity in the church is not only morally correct but is increasingly becoming a matter of survival for many congregations. Some churches prefer closing their doors to integrating along racial lines, it seems. In fact, many of those churches have been sold to a faith community of a different ethnicity. All across the U.S., churches are closing, partly because of their refusal to promote racial unity in sacred places, and even as churches go extinct, the dominant body of literature is inattentive to this development.

Another challenge to church diversity is cultural conflict, which occurs when two or more cultures disagree to the point of harboring emotional resentment, engaging in verbal or physical assault, or refusing to work together to achieve goals. Emotional resentment does not have to lead to verbal assault, but it can occur in faith communities. Regardless of all efforts to conceal it, emotional resentment is nearly impossible to keep secret forever. Church members can harbor ill feelings against other members when they perceive the other group is receiving favoritism, displaying indifference, or is in total command of the happenings of the church. Emotional resentment from one group of church members will eventually become evident by their actions: not supporting the church financially and not having a sense of ownership. Brian Bantum insightfully observes how race often impacts personhood:

> Race is a phenomenon of racial performance that forms disciples. Race is not merely a form of social organization, but more significantly a form of religious expression and identity that shape who a person is. But race as a system of belief also indicates more than who a person

87

> is. Structures of racial formation articulate the telos of
> the inhabitant's life, what she will live into, and what she
> will not. In this regard race becomes a category that or-
> ganizes and guides the very presumptions people make
> about themselves and their world. However, this perfor-
> mance of race remains, the ways it is lived into and acted
> out of, hidden even in the midst of competing visions
> of racial life.[2]

The clergyperson in some cross-racial pastoral cases should be
mindful that some members will be watchful, sensitive, and ready
to complain about any perceived notions of pastoral favoritism
toward any group of people. Pastoral favoritism can occur with
people of the clergyperson's own ethnicity or people of a different
ethnicity. Clergy need to make it clear by word and behavior that
they practice nondiscriminatory and nonpreferential leadership.

In multicultural church ministry, all members ought to be
conscious of the power dynamics and should be attentive to how
they are welcoming or not welcoming other groups into the fabric of their church life. Too often multicultural churches function
similar to tenants in an apartment building: they all live in the
same building and their goal is not to commit any offenses against
one another. One tenant goes one way and another tenant goes
a different way, and occasionally they cross paths. Multicultural
church ministry should function at a much higher level of interaction. All groups share the responsibility of including the other
in religious celebrations, rituals, and joys and concerns. Do not
allow language barriers to be an excuse for not getting to know one
another at a deeper spiritual level. Millions of people who speak
different languages, including church folk, take part in meaningful
secular activities such as athletic events, shopping, house services,
music, and dance; language barriers do not prevent them from
participating. It is ironic that cultural conflict does not seem to
occur in such secular events at the same rate or intensity as it does
in religious situations.

2. Bantum, *Redeeming Mulatto*, 19.

A verbal assault within a church context is not solely when one person uses harsh language toward another person. In diverse church settings, verbal assaults generally occur when a group of people become condescending toward another group of people, or use accusatory language against others within the church community. Bantum explains,

> In modernity, race disciplined our lives and structured our hopes. It was not God. Race subtly marked the rhythm of our speech and the shape of our lips, granting us access into one space and obstructing our passage into another. It is these patterns of exclusion and entrance that continue to mark the church today and it is these patterns that must die. Mulatto/Christian bodies ask the church to reflect upon the desires that lead to separate languages, services, and distinctions between styles, resisting the migrant worker among them or refusing the discomfort of entering into the struggle for a life beyond the veil of color.[3]

In cross-racial pastoral ministry, the clergyperson should especially refrain from speaking in terms of "us versus them" and should monitor their tone in conversations. Cultures tend to communicate differently in terms of pitch, word choice, and body language. Clergypersons need to have a high level of social intelligence as it relates to leading a congregation of another ethnicity. They should be willing to learn from books, mentoring, conferences, workshops, and classes about pastoral leadership in various church contexts. Laypeople examine their pastor closely, even when they appear not to be paying much attention. Most people can innately detect when another person is uncomfortable or oblivious, in almost any setting. Clergypersons in a cross-racial pastoral ministry need to be conscious of their setting so that they can lead the faith community in progressive ways that will be pleasing to God.

It is easy for members of different cultures to misunderstand and misinterpret each other's messages. In multicultural church situations, members should also be especially attentive to how they

3. Ibid., 192.

speak to one another and their pastor. Careful communication can result in members avoiding pointless anger and preventing unnecessary opposition. It is possible for the members of one ethnicity to confuse or antagonize their pastor of a different ethnicity through miscommunication. In diverse church settings, conflict generally occurs when a group of people ridicule or act inhospitably toward another group of people.

PASTORAL IMAGES AND PERCEPTIONS

The United States has a long and complex history of discrimination against people of color. In fact, the church in the U.S. has been one of the major perpetrators of the many injustices against vulnerable populations. To be fair, the church has also been an advocate for people in need; but, like most organizations, the church has always been in need of improvement, especially when it comes to aspects of diversity.

Pastoral images are influential in church settings. In cross-racial pastoral cases, clergy should be mindful of how their physical presence is being perceived. Ideally, the clergyperson will always be perceived as pastoral, but most people know that that is not always the case. For example, during my first six months to a year of any pastoral ministry, I frequently wear a priestly collar during religious services and pastoral visitations. It is important for the clergyperson to be easily identifiable by everyone in cross-racial pastoral ministry. This practice has been valuable for me in a variety of settings, such as church and hospital, when I could easily be mistaken as a person serving in a role other than a pastoral one.

In cross-racial pastoral situations, many of the laity may not be able to see their clergyperson as a reflection of themselves. If their pastor were of the same race, laypeople, consciously or unconsciously, might simply look upon her as a daughter or sister or some other family member. But cross-racial pastoral situations can be more complex, as a clergyperson from a different ethnicity may represent a variety of images far from priestly in the minds of laypeople who are mostly of a different ethnicity. I have had several discussions with clergy from various Asian backgrounds, and many have shared stories of initial conversations with members in which the members expressed to them unflattering recollections related to the Korean War, Vietnam War, or the U.S. military presence in the Philippines. These mostly negative first impressions or first conversations can come from any layperson of any cultural background. In these situations, the parishioners' first instinct is to associate the clergyperson with a former national enemy, rather than embracing their clergyperson as their very own pastor to love, to be loved by, and to pray for in this process of becoming increasingly faithful disciples of Jesus Christ in ways that glorify God.

In some multicultural church ministry, groups of people may have a long history of serious conflicts with one another, which can be embedded in their subconscious. Church members may not be fully aware of their suspicion or dislike of each other or of their pastor. This could be their first genuine or ongoing interaction with one another. This interaction can take place along lines of race, class, gender, and many other identity markers. When church folk are unfamiliar with one another they may foster uncomplimentary sentiments. Unfortunately, they may distance themselves from one another rather than viewing one another as extensions of themselves in order to care for one another. An unattached (injured) body part cannot care for itself properly: when the shoulder is dislocated, it cannot heal itself. In multicultural ministry, there should be some important areas where the body of Jesus Christ can come together to touch and agree by the power of the Holy Spirit; this coming together will not be easy, however, as Soong-Chan Rah observes: "The idealism and optimism of developing multiethnic congregations, however, is being replaced by frustration and pessimism as the difficult reality of multiethnic ministry becomes more and more apparent. To reverse centuries of negative history between the races and to rectify ignorance and incompetence when it comes to cross-cultural sensitivity is not an easy task."[4]

4. Rah, *Many Colors*, 11.

I have always been aware of my identity as an African-American pastor of predominantly Caucasian churches. A very wise mentor of mine suggested that I allow myself to become my congregation's pastor in every way, regardless of the congregation's ethnicity. The same mentor elaborated on the importance of not disqualifying myself from being able to pastor beyond racial or national categories. My mentor discussed the many occasions when clergy were unable to pastor in certain church settings because of their own personal restrictions along racial or national lines. There's a good deal of validity in the old adage that "most limitations in life we place on ourselves." Clergy, especially pastors in cross-racial contexts, must culturally liberate themselves before they can help lead a congregation to go beyond ethnic boundaries.

Pastoral perceptions are significant in faith communities, especially in church settings. Most religious groups have preconceived images and notions when it comes to the preferable attributes of their clergy. For example, some congregations seek clergy based on education level, number of quality of internships, gender, or ethnicity. When a church perceives a certain demographic as nonpastoral or even dangerous, it is unlikely that a cross-racial pastoral ministry will ever occur or succeed. There is a long history of minorities being portrayed as unintelligent, criminal, nonreligious, and immoral. These negative portrayals help create stereotypes and prejudices in church communities that too often lead to discrimination.

IDENTITY CRISIS AND TERRITORIAL CONFLICT

A common challenge to church diversity is identity crisis, which happens when the majority (in terms of membership, money, or power) is threatened by the perceived or real change of the congregation's demographics; the congregation fears being transformed into a faith community of a different ethnicity. One unfortunate outcome of such fear is white flight—a large number of Caucasians leave a community because of the arrival of people of color. To combat this fear, says Rah, "The church needs to develop cultural intelligence in order to fully realize the many-colored tapestry that God is weaving together. . . . In other words, it does not help us to be culturally blind when developing multi-cultural ministry."[5]

An identity crisis may occur for a variety of reasons. The negative polarization of race in the mainstream media does not help matters. It makes sense that some congregations would be hesitant to hire clergy of a different race. People of all races can find excuses not to accept those of other races as members of their churches. Suspicions can run high for all parties. Yet and still, a good topic for exploraton and research is why, in most multicultural ministries, the senior pastor is Caucasian. People of color are more prone (or expected) to join a church with a Caucasian senior pastor. Why does it seem unacceptable among most Caucasian laity to have a clergyperson of color, especially as the senior pastor? Identity crisis plays a role in preventing individuals and congregations from becoming more racially inclusive. It also causes members of the same race in a faith community to experience discomfort when a clergyperson of a different gender assumes the role of senior pastor. Identity crisis prevents individuals and congregations from becoming more inclusive when it comes to race, gender, sexual orientation, and class.

An identity crisis within a faith community may occur for several different reasons—for example, when a church experiences an unexpected increase of diversity in its worship attendance, changing demographics in its membership, or greater diversity in its lay leadership or pastoral leadership. This can result in uncertainties about the future as it relates to diversity. An identity crisis may also occur when a church grieves the loss of who it perceived itself to be, and realizes that it does not fit that image anymore; this can generate feelings of shame along with grave doubts about the future. An identity crisis may cause a church to experience internal strife in the form of finger-pointing and accusations, a struggle for power, or the lack of a decisive leadership direction. In 2009, the *New York Times* reported on one such internal conflict, at the fabled Riverside Church in New York City:

5. Ibid., 12.

Since its founding in 1930 as a Gothic cathedral built by John D. Rockefeller, Riverside Church has espoused a progressive and often pacifist agenda. But internal fights have plagued the congregation for more than a decade. Longtime members ascribe some of the tension to changes in the racial makeup of the 2,700-member congregation, which was once about 60 percent white and 40 percent black, and now is roughly the reverse. Some of the troubles are traced to generational differences, between older whites with roots in the civil rights era and younger, middle-class black members who are less politicized.[6]

One example of a cross-racial pastoral ministry is when a clergyperson of one race becomes senior pastor of a congregation whose membership is predominantly of a different race. Sometimes the reaction is a sense of panic. This panic can overtake a congregation if its members think that the floodgates will open overnight and a host of people of the same race as the senior pastor will commandeer the church. Too often, church members are more concerned about being known primarily as a church of a particular racial or ethnic group, rather than being known primarily as followers of Jesus Christ. It is not unheard of for church members to be adamant about keeping their faith community closed to whoever they perceive as outsiders. These individuals may be open to diversity, but only as long as it does not compromise their personal comfort zones.

An identity crisis can lead to territorial conflict. In church settings, territorial conflict occurs when one person or group of people within a faith community lays claim to ownership or control of the congregation. There are quite a few Christian congregations in the U.S. who share facilities with an immigrant faith community. The immigrant congregation usually conducts their worship service on a different day or at a different time from the predominantly American congregation. Rarely do the congregations worship together or participate together in other church-related activities such as education programs, mission trips,

6. Vitello, "Riverside Church Pastor Resigns."

finances, and leadership. Frequently, the immigrant group pays a fee for building use to the predominantly American congregation. In other cases, congregations of different ethnicities are directed by their denomination to share one church building in an attempt to conserve limited financial resources. Inevitably, one or all participating congregations will experience territorial conflict. In May 2013, the *Washington Post* reported on conflict at Washington, DC's First Baptist Church:

> Baptists, along with other mainstream American denominations, still struggle with the nation's legacy of racism and segregation, and the ministry of a black pastor to head a historically white congregation was a rare occurrence. Now, the bitter ending has made some urban pastors uneasy. In the turmoil at First Baptist, they recognize familiar themes of race, power and angst over how to reverse declining membership at U.S. houses of worship. "What happens when you call a leader and that leader fosters diversity and then the congregation says, 'Whoa, we don't want to go'?" said Ricky Creech, head of the District of Columbia Baptist Convention, a racially diverse group of area Baptist churches, and a longtime church consultant. "You can have diversity on a bus but not all be going to the same location."[7]

I pastored a multicultural church consisting of four congregations: American (comprised of various ethnicities), Korean-American, Spanish-American, and Filipino-American. All four congregations had different worship times on Sunday, separate budgets, and programs unique to their membership. We had a few worship services together during the year and participated in a number of mutually beneficial endeavors. When relations were good, it was heavenly. When relations were bad, it was hell. In good times, the theme was "We are all one big family, all God's children!" In bad times, the theme was "This is my church—get out!" From time to time each congregation would claim exclusive ownership of the church building and want to try to remove the others. Territorial

---

7. Harris and Boorstein, "Dismal Parting."

conflict can occur in regard to the sanctuary, kitchen, fellowship hall, gym, baptismal pool, or any other area of the church. This can lead to resentment, anger, and a system that is unhealthy for the entire congregation, especially the children, who may grow up feeling inferior to other people or superior to other people.

Ultimately, of course, the congregation is God's. This declaration needs to be conveyed on paper, read aloud, and spoken publicly and privately. Many profound messages are hardly ever written on paper, read aloud, or spoken publicly and privately, and yet they are sent and received loud and clear. Church business should be God's business, so we need to give the appropriate time, seriousness, and resources to this spiritual enterprise.

In cross-racial pastoral ministry, it is important for the clergyperson to understand that the church more than likely opened its doors long before their approval. Furthermore, the church will most likely remain after her pastoral ministry ends. It is a waste of valuable energy, time, and social capital for the clergyperson to engage in unimportant battles. Energy, time, and social capital are best used in strategic partnerships and collaborative meetings for the common good. Of course, disagreements may arise, but it is wise for any clergyperson to realize it may take time for church members to wholeheartedly trust new pastoral leadership decisions related to the properties and assets they acquired long before the pastoral ministry assignment was made. I am not advocating for clergypersons in cross-racial pastoral ministry to shrink from their pastoral authority. Instead, I am suggesting that those clergypersons understand how race can polarizes any issue, especially in church. Therefore, a greater sensitivity in decision-making should be applied by and for all parties involved—clergy and laity alike.

There tends to be a premature notion that the appointment of a clergyperson of a given race will lead, almost overnight, to a change in the racial makeup of the church's membership. It is likely that people of the new pastor's race will not be quick to attend or join the church, for a variety of reasons: the church's inability to bring in or keep new members, or church politics, or the reputation of the church among the residents of the neighborhood. Jennings acknowledges the dynamic challenges as "people defined by their cultural differences yet who turn their histories and cultural logics toward a new determination, a new social performance of identity."[8] It is good for clergy to be aware of how pastoral presence can impact the identity of any church in minor or major ways. Churches are referred to as having a female pastor, a military chaplain pastor, a legally blind pastor, a pastor with a DMin or PhD, a pastor with impressive musical skills, a young pastor, or a physically disabled pastor. It is imperative for the clergyperson to be fairly confident in who she is and who she is not. This confidence and pastoral stability can be a major factor in directing the congregation out of identity-crisis mode into a mode of security.

CHURCH LEADERSHIP

As I have suggested throughout this book, Church leadership is essential to greater church diversity. Today Christianity is in dire need of serious leadership in relation to diversity, both among ordained clergy and the laity. There should be effective pastoral leaders and lay leaders whose responsibility it is to increase church diversity in the form of cross-racial pastoral ministry and multicultural ministry. Historically, God has empowered and relied on leaders to do noble yet difficult work, and now is no different. The world can be burdensome, and too often different members of humanity are bitterly divided over petty details, but God is using some pastors and parishioners to bring a greater level of diversity in harmonious ways. There *are* cases of cross-racial pastoral ministry and multicultural ministry occurring in the U.S.; unfortunately, they are the exception rather than the rule. Who is helping prepare a new generation of church leadership—people of all ages, cultures, and genders—for the glory of God? The entire church should be asking this question on behalf of the future of the church and future generations. Leaders should be concerned

8. Jennings, *Christian Imagination*, 273.

not only about the present; they should also plan for the future. A superb example of a leader's mature outlook toward the future can be found in the following Old Testament passage:

> Moses said to the LORD, "May the LORD, the God of the spirits of all mankind, appoint a man over this community to go out and come in before them, one who will lead them out and bring them in, so the LORD's people will not be like sheep without a shepherd." So the LORD said to Moses, "Take Joshua son of Nun, a man in whom is the spirit, and lay your hand on him." (Num 27:15–18)

This illustrates the importance of church leadership for the continuity for God's people. In this passage, God specifically instructed Moses to perform a religious ceremony, which many people would associate with an ordination, special blessing, or commissioning to do a special ministry. Having persons set aside for specific tasks remains important today. Here's an example that illustrates the importance of leadership in Jesus's eyes:

> Jesus went through all the towns and villages, teaching in their synagogues, preaching the good news of the kingdom and healing every disease and sickness. When he saw the crowds, he had compassion on them, because they were harassed and helpless, like sheep without a shepherd. Then he said to his disciples, "The harvest is plentiful but the workers are few. Ask the Lord of the harvest, therefore, to send out workers into his harvest field." (Matt 9:35–38)

Jesus acknowledged the importance of having someone set aside as a shepherd. God provides ways and means for people to accept leadership responsibilities in religious contexts.

Church leadership has been passed down from generation to generation through the Holy Spirit. Leadership is usually mysterious and miraculous, especially in sacred spaces. Leadership roles are essential to a congregation's mission and everyday operations. Pastors and parishioners need one another. There needs to be generations of people who are systematically mentored for church leadership at every level in Christianity. Will Willimon notes,

The central liturgical gesture of ordination is the laying on of hands, a sign that is full of significance for clergy. There is in this gesture a conferral of power and authority from those who have borne this burden to those newly called to lead. Any authority and power that clergy have is never our own; it is a gift, bestowal from the Holy Spirit and the church. Though most of us today associate the laying on of hands with ordination, it is a baptismal gesture. When used in ordination, the laying on of hands is a sign that the call to ministry is preceded by the baptismal call and arises out of the general ministry of all Christians in baptism.[9]

Many faith communities have components of mentorship and supervision. Depending on the particular denomination, people are taught or indoctrinated into the faith before baptism, confirmation, and/or church membership. What messages are faith communities sending to younger generations? What messages are faith communities not sending to younger generations? Every faith group under the Christian banner is in need of competent leadership, and Willimon's descriptions through a theological perspective celebrate the gift of ordination. All Christians should look at all leadership opportunities as splendid ways to be present in the world. An ordained person is not expected to be flawless in her Christian community, but she is expected to be renewed while serving as a catalyst for Christian living in spirit and in truth. Willimon notes,

It is not that the pastor is expected to be a morally more exemplary Christian than other Christians, but rather that pastors are expected to act in a way that befits their public and communal, that is, churchly, obligations. Note that 1 Timothy has no qualms about linking a pastor's public, congregational role with the pastor's responsibility toward marriage and family. Clearly, pastors are to be role models for the church, without that troublesome

9. Willimon, *Pastor*, 48–49.

modern separation between public and private, social and personal, behavior.[10]

Congregations and the world are in need of leaders who are willing to be set apart to do the work that God has assigned them. Effective church leaders find value in constantly reading books and studying historical literature about former leaders to seek advice and insight. These persons will not take their leadership tasks lightly; they will embrace their responsibility to God and God's creation to do their best and be their best.

Church leaders come in all shapes, sizes, and races—and, not surprisingly, with different assumptions and attitudes. All church leaders should consider whether or not they will strategically lead their faith communities to a greater level of church diversity. In all situations, leaders should lead. Too many church leaders are evading church diversity because they lack courage and initiative. Many congregations have been disappointed in their pastors and other church leaders because they are not performing better in the area of race relations. These congregations are waiting for their pastors and lay leaders to help improve church diversity. Will more pastors and lay leaders help increase church diversity? Are the majority of pastors and lay leaders waiting for their congregations to unanimously tell them or give them permission to advance church diversity? Willimon writes, "One great difference between a pastor and other givers of care in society is that a pastor can take initiative and intrude into the troubled lives of his or her people. It is part of a pastor's role not simply to wait until hurting people reach out for help, but also to seek out and save the lost."[11]

Church leadership brings forth an abundance of excitement and opportunities. Church leadership has the responsibility to continue to lead God's children out of bondage regardless of the people's desire or willingness. In both the Old Testament and New Testament, many people complained and groaned during the process of being liberated by their religious leadership.

10. Ibid., 45.
11. Ibid., 104.

SOME POSSIBLE CHALLENGES

Personally, I consider my role in church leadership one of my highest honors and one of my biggest challenges. Of course, I consider my educational degrees and community service awards noble, perhaps even impressive, but for me secular accolades are not comparable to church leadership. There is a lifelong work given to church leaders, whether ordained or nonordained. Unfortunately, too many people become comfortable in church leadership roles among people who behave; believe, and look very much like them. Perhaps this is understandable; when we examine the historical record, we see there are reasons for wariness and even mistrust between different cultures, which may hamper increasing church diversity in the form of cross-racial pastoral ministry and multicultural ministry.

In the U.S. historically, the two largest and most prominent racial groups have been Caucasian-Americans (people of European descent) and African-Americans (people of African descent). Their significant religious activities in the form of denominations, colleges, and universities, as well as civic engagement, have been well documented. The conflicts between the two groups have likewise been well documented and continue to be a source of animosity, resentment, and mistrust. H. Leon McBeth writes, "The American churches were slow to evangelize among the blacks, partly from language barriers and partly from a prejudice among some who doubted whether blacks had souls to be saved. Some slave owners also hesitated because of economic concern; an ancient tradition asserted that a slave converted could no longer be held in servitude, having become a brother in Christ. However, by 1660 Colonial legislatures had passed laws that Christian conversion did not affect the outward state or condition of slaves."[12]

From the days before the creation of the United States, Christians in the U.S. have tried to unite with one another on a daily or weekly basis in the form of congregational life; they continue to do so. Various cultures have tried to get along with one another in this world since the days of antiquity; unfortunately, we have been unsuccessful. Disharmony is not foreign to any religion, and

12. McBeth, *Baptist Heritage*, 776.

Christianity is of course no exception. Jesus' first disciples and earliest apostles did not always get along but frequently argued. However, one of the mandates in Christianity is to love; Jesus said, "So now I am giving you a new commandment: Love each other. Just as I have loved you, you should love each other" (John 13:34). Despite Jesus's words, a great number of Christians in the U.S. have endeavored to treat other Christians in unfair, unethical, and unlawful ways. This maltreatment has shaped the religious landscape in America as people, especially African-Americans, have fled churches to start their own; to quote McBeth again,

> How to relate to white Baptists has been a persistent question for black Baptists in America. Many early black churches affiliated with predominantly white associations, while others pioneered in founding black associations. After 1865 most black Baptists withdrew from white churches to form their own, and formation of the National Baptist Convention in 1895 provided their own general body. [13]

Many people of color decided to form their own denominations because of the white church's exclusionary practices. Religious communities have helped create some criminally systematic and institutionalized forms of racism, such as the Ku Klux Klan, Jim Crow laws, and lynching. Unfortunately, hostile memories linger and some of discriminatory practices can be seen even today. Racial and cultural reconciliation has been a long and a difficult journey. To be accurate and fair, however, many discriminatory practices were simultaneously opposed by many faith communities; there were instances when individuals bravely stood up against discrimination to promote equality when their own religious communities were enforcing various forms of prejudice.

A challenge for many congregations is their lack of knowledge of their own history. In the U.S., race and culture usually have determined whether one could gain entry into the membership of a congregation. Consequently, minorities were often denied entry into a white congregation, on multiple levels. Still and all,

13. McBeth, *Baptist Heritage*, 789.

the majority of African-Americans and other minorities continued to remain Christian rather than turning to other religions. Christian congregations in the U.S. have not been ideal, but they have managed to make steps toward progress in some areas. The Methodists, for example, have experienced several organizational transformations, such as divisions, splits, and growth. In *The Story of American Methodism*, Frederick A. Norwood notes that in 1900 there were more than seven different denominations within Methodism.[14] One of the goals of Methodism in the past, which still continues today in some of its circles, is to unite all the schisms of Methodism as one body. This goal has yet to be reached. Historically, the different denominations within Methodism were divided primarily by two issues: theology and race (especially race). Today, race and culture are the two primary factors that still divide Christian congregations.

In 1939 a union was created to bring together the Methodist Protestant Church, the Methodist Episcopal Church, and the Methodist Episcopal Church South, to allow these churches to share resources and expand the reach of the denomination. While the churches in this union agreed on the need to consolidate their efforts to continue to grow, they did not agree on the issue of race relations. Unfortunately during that time, African-American Methodists were put in the "other" category by the majority of white Methodists, creating walls of division in the Wesleyan tradition. Many African-Americans chose to join African-American Methodist denominations such as the African Methodist Episcopal (A.M.E.), Methodist Episcopal (M.E.), African Methodist Episcopal Zion (A.M.E.Z.), and Colored Methodist Episcopal (C.M.E.) churches. A smaller number of African-Americans stayed within the predominantly white Methodist Church, being hopeful of social change. To address the issue of race within the Methodist Church, in 1939 the union created the Central Jurisdiction—a conference designed solely for African-American Methodist membership. The creation of the Central Jurisdiction was an illustration

14. Norwood, *Story of American Methodism*, 359.

of a denomination not leading or setting a proper humanitarian example for the world to follow.

In regard to race relations, the Methodist Church, along with other faith communities, was tarnishing its reputation, and it faced criticism from people who opposed discrimation within religious life. Methodists' opinions varied widely about the creation of the Central Jurisdiction among the African-Americans who were supposed to "benefit" from the exclusionary practice. African-Americans generally accepted it as both a blessing and a curse. This new jurisdiction would allow, for the first time, all African-Americans to serve in essential church leadership positions that were never before offered to them within the denomination. This opportunity was also seen as a curse because it was yet another example of racial discrimination toward people of African descent within the same denomination in which they chose to worship. Caucasians generally saw the Central Jurisdiction as a step of progress toward the ultimate goal of unifying Methodism. However, some Caucasians did acknowledge the shadow of blatant alienation amongst fellow Christians.

With all the "positives" the Central Jurisdiction offered African-Americans in the Methodist Church, it could not dispel the shadows within the Christian community. Most African-Americans protested their subordinate membership, and some Caucasians agreed to help them eliminate this unfair segregation within the denomination. As a result, efforts were put forth to find a way to end this specific type of segregation within their religious denomination, which lasted for more than twenty-five years. Thomas notes, "The Central Jurisdiction was heavily opposed by the African-American members of the Uniting Conference in 1939. But once the structure was in place, the members of the nineteen annual conferences decided to use it as best as they could, until such time as the racial jurisdiction could be abolished."[15]

The separation between the churches was eliminated with the merger of the Central Jurisdiction into the Methodist Church and ultimately the 1968 union, which was an example of the Wesleyan

15. Thomas, *Methodism's Racial Dilemma*, 170.

tradition striving for more unity within the church for all believers of the gospel of Jesus Christ. This union dissolved the Central Jurisdiction, a giant leap toward equality; but the changes it required were a challenge that took time and commitment from those involved. African-Americans and Caucasians in the Methodist Church could no longer love one another from a distance. They had to come to terms with each other's humanity in a more personal way within Methodism before they could eventually make another progressive transformation into the United Methodist Church (UMC). The UMC as we know it today emerged from the 1968 unification of the Methodist Church and the Evangelical United Brethren Church.

In order for all Christian denominations to continue to move forward in race and culture relations, they must abide by the message God gave Moses: "Never seek revenge or bear a grudge against anyone, but love your neighbor as yourself. I am the LORD" (Lev 19:18). Currently, congregations in the U.S. have an awesome opportunity to learn from past conflicts and resolutions, as well as from those who championed equality. One such figure was Ida B. Wells-Barnett, who was raised in a local Methodist Episcopal Church and attended one of its schools of higher education, Rust College. In the early 1900s, she undoubtedly helped set a tone of racial justice in American society. She spent an enormous amount of time traveling across America giving lectures to numerous organizations in favor of equal rights for people of African descent. In a 1903 lecture titled "The Colored Woman, Her Past, Present and Future," delivered to the Political Equality League, Wells-Barnett noted that "there was little employment for the Negro, and the average Negro scarcely exceeded the domestic scale." After the white listeners responded with expressions of sympathy, Wells-Barnett answered, "We ask only that the door of opportunity be opened to us."[16]

Christian communities are not exempt from imperfection. They should always make strides toward improvement. Many African-Americans have felt as though their prayerful persistence

16. Keller, *Spirituality and Social Responsibility*, 153.

PRACTICAL THEOLOGY FOR CHURCH DIVERSITY

delivered them from inequality into opportunity and fairness. Not only did Wells-Barnett speak out against injustices but she also spoke out against specific people. Her actions are well documented:

> In 1909, Wells-Barnett led the fight against the reinstatement of Frank Davis as Sheriff in Alexander County, Illinois. Davis had allowed a black to be lynched in Cairo, Illinois. Under Illinois law this was neglect of his duties. After investigating the incident in Cairo, Wells-Barnett brought out the facts of the case and, in a bitter fight, presented her case to Governor Charles Deneen. He subsequently refused to reinstate Sheriff Davis despite heavy political pressure on Davis' behalf. Wells-Barnett was succinct in stating her conclusion of the effect of the case: "From that day until the present there has been no lynching in the state."[17]

Wells-Barnett, along with the work of several females in American culture, helped ignite a moral consciousness within the Methodist community that is still visible today.

One may ask the question, Why did most minorities continue to stay within Christian faith communities during years of discomfort and discrimination? A small number of minorities did abandon Christianity because they could not remain a Christian under discrimination, prejudice, and racism. Most minorities, however, remained within their Christian community, whether Methodist, Baptist, Catholic, or other.

Minorities have made significant theological contributions to Christianity in the U.S. One way they responded to the harsh conditions within Christianity in the U.S. was by writing life-giving material that spoke to their experiences. James Cone writes, "All creative Christian theologies come into being as persons encounter contradictions in life about which they cannot be silent. . . . We had to speak out or there would be no way we could defend ourselves against black power advocates' claims that Christianity is a white religion. Just as Luther spoke of 'the Babylonian captivity of the church,' attacking the doctrine of seven sacraments, we saw

17. Ibid.

a similar analogy with the white church, enslaved, as it was, by its own racism."[18]

Theologians such as James Cone have helped minorities re-examine their practices and remain Christian. Many minorities have made great strides in reinterpreting their harsh conditions through mediums such as literature and songs. Cain Hope Felder writes, "I began to realize that my own theological training and graduate studies had treated most of ancient Africa as peripheral or insignificant. I also recognized that aspects of European his-toriography and archeology have been tainted by a self-serving, racialist hermeneutic that sought not objective truth but careful, 'scientific' ways of reinforcing the superiority and normative char-acter of Western culture (i.e., white people) as the sole arbitrator of the biblical tradition."[19]

African-Americans and other minorities helped create goals and objectives through various coalitions within Christian com-munities to ensure equality for all cultures within faith communi-ties. Fortunately, these individuals have accepted one of church leadership's sacred responsibilities: to serve in increasing church diversity on multiple levels.

Some Christian communities have done better than others in improving their religious landscape. Progress should always be acknowledged and celebrated for purposes of education, informa-tion, and inspiration. If faith communities are not aware of what has been done in the past in relation to church diversity, it will be difficult for them to understand the road ahead. Jean Miller Schmidt writes, "Quakers, Congregationalists, Unitarians and Universalists, and Freewill Baptists had been among the earliest religious groups in the United States to grant women the right to preach. All were characterized by either Free Church polity or a stress on empowerment by God's indwelling Spirit. In 1853 An-toinette Brown was ordained to a small Congregational Church

18. Cone, *For My People*, 41.
19. Felder, *Troubling Biblical Waters*, 8.

in South Butler, New York; she was probably the first ordained woman minister in America."[20]

There is no perfect faith community, of course; there never has been. All progress comes to communities after a great deal of sacrifice—of time, energy, resources, relationships, and reputation. There is a countless number of Christians who loved their faith community so much that they were willing to help make their congregation better for everyone. A challenge that many congregations have is to not become pessimistic about what still is possible in the form of church diversity. Another challenge is to not underestimate the work required to help prepare a congregation for a cross-racial pastoral ministry and a greater multicultural ministry. Soong-Chan Rah writes, "The work of cross-cultural ministry is a difficult one. If the task of building a multiethnic church were an easy one, then every church in America could be experiencing the joys of successful multicultural ministry. . . . The deeply seated demonic power of racism cannot be overthrown without great cost."[21]

Prejudice and racism are learned behaviors and deeply embedded in any community. Yet, those exclusionary practices can also be much more than behavior learned from a relative or a friend. A challenge for many Christians is to not take too lightly Jesus' description of the enemy's mission as "to kill, steal, and destroy" (John 10:10). Congregations' efforts to increase church diversity through cross-racial pastoral ministry and multicultural ministry are serious business. Sometimes it is more than simply "this is just how we are and how we do things around here." Sometimes congregations have been victims of the evil that divides humanity in nearly everything. The challenges are major, yes, but the solutions are possible; it starts with all of us.

20. Schmidt, *Grace Sufficient*, 196.
21. Rah, *Many Colors*, 196.

6

Possible Solutions and Extra Miles

SCENARIO #1

EVERYONE WAS HAVING A wonderful time talking, laughing, and dancing in the elaborately decorated room where the bride and groom had spent several months choosing wedding colors, music, and seating arrangements. All the people who truly mattered to the beautiful bride and handsome groom were present. Their supportive family and friends were in attendance, surrounding them with love and giving congratulatory handshakes, hugs, kisses, and well wishes. The celebrated couple did not realize who was absent from their wedding activities, nor did they care one iota. Much like the membership of their church, those attending the ceremony and reception were predominantly of one ethnicity. For a variety of reasons, moments like this one seem to illuminate cross-racial pastoral ministry. Wedding ceremonies tend to have more visitors that fly in from across the country than the average Sunday worship service. The pastor usually stands closer to the congregation and declares sacred words to the couple, family, and congregation. The photography and video cameras will include the pastor as a special person in the wedding ceremony for many years.

The young couple did notice a question directed at them from a coworker they both considered a friend. Their friend politely asked,

"Why did you not inform me that your new pastor is of a different ethnicity from ours? I have never had a pastor from a totally different culture. You never shared this information with me! I understand your pastor has been here for a few years now. How is it? What's it like?" The couple paused briefly, then responded, "We never told you or anyone else that we have a new pastor of a different ethnicity because we have always felt we simply have a new pastor. We always think the pastor of our congregation is the best, and that has not changed! Our current pastor is similar to our previous pastors in the sense that we deeply cherish the pastoral leadership role."

The above scenario describes a common dialogue related to cross-racial pastoral ministry. It will be nice when questions about differences related to cultural diversity within congregations will not have to be asked with such curiosity, because it will have become the norm. This chapter offers practical approaches to addressing the challenges mentioned in earlier chapters. Techniques for good communication, church leadership diplomacy, and other activities are necessary for church diversity. People are passionate about what they hold sacred; church is one place where tempers, voices, and emotions may rise, and strong opinions may form, because people may not agree with the actions of their religious community. Challenges will arise, but by relying on God and working with one another in strategic ways, solutions are possible.

Religion at its best brings people together in harmonious ways, facilitates healing, and conveys meaning. Paul L. Lehmann asks, "What am I, as a believer in Jesus Christ and as a member of his church, to do?"[1] Lehmann's emphasis on questioning the member's role in church is noteworthy; he presses church members to ponder and respond to their relationship to Jesus Christ in tangible ways within their faith community. It can be difficult for Christians to identify the ways in which they hinder, impede, and nullify progress. It is too easy for people, including Christians, to focus more on challenges than on solutions. One reason it is difficult is that people have deep-seated emotions, and feelings they are

1. Lehmann, *Ethics in a Christian Context*, 25.

not even aware of, relating to identity, fear, and prejudice. Religion at its worst separates people, devastates people, and leads people into despair. Going the extra miles includes constantly expanding the church community to take account of all God's children, because we are responsible for all of our neighbors. The Lord's Prayer begins with the words "Our Father," and the word *our* points to the need for us to go beyond our familiarities, culture, and traditions.

One reason why going the extra miles is not easy is that people and organizations usually stop when they have not made any progress. Working on the road toward church diversity can be exhausting, and many travelers find plenty of reasons to make a U-turn—or they actually jump off the bus when they feel church diversity within their congregation has surpassed their limits. I need to warn you that participating in the quest for church diversity is countercultural in more than a few places in the U.S. Going the extra miles, people of faith are challenged to become active participants rather than passive bystanders. The world is in need of a church that will do more than shake your hand, sing a hymn, preach a sermon, and then send you away.

A special emphasis on finding solutions is essential; an incoming clergyperson should get in the habit of seeking potential solutions. Some people will question the value of church diversity, and they may even have supposedly biblical arguments against it; the truth is that the Bible cannot be intelligently used to defend a lack of church diversity. It is important for Christians to know, and have the ability to articulate, all the reasons why they are involved and invested in church diversity.

The moral case alone does not seem to cause hearts, minds, and souls to change. If morality were a major deciding factor, then many dire situations would not occur. Christians come from different life experiences and points of view, and the acknowledgment of sin seems to have little influence on how people prefer to operate their church. This is evident in both overt and covert discriminatory procedures in churches throughout the U.S. Other strategies must be utilized in order to foster successful cross-racial pastoral ministry and multicultural ministry.

COMMUNICATION TECHNIQUES TO RESOLVE CULTURAL CONFLICT

Communication is vital and can be a major contributing factor of failure or success in any organization, especially in a church setting. The pastor is looked upon as the main communicator within a faith community. Parishioners look forward to communicating with their pastor during worship services, counseling sessions, celebrations, Bible studies, and funeral services. Another occasion when clergy ought to be willing and able to communicate effectively is during cultural conflict. In cross-racial pastoral ministry, clergypersons need to be cognizant of their church context. Clergy should intentionally select the optimal communication style in the midst of cultural conflict. Additionally, it should be the shared responsibility of pastors and parishioners to help alleviate and eliminate cultural conflict when it arises in their church setting. There are three recommended communication roles to resolve cultural conflict: the primary listener, the primary facilitator, and the primary negotiator.

The Primary Listener

Church has a peculiar language for a peculiar people. Most communities, whether religious or secular, have their own language that is uniquely theirs. For most church members, words such as God, Jesus Christ, Holy Spirit, Christmas, Lent, the cross, resurrection, Easter, baptism, sin, forgiveness, and redemption take on special meaning. How can Christians not worship together in spirit and in truth on a weekly basis when they speak the same language and profess the same beliefs? Duke Divinity School Professor Willie Jennings thinks the separation is obvious: "Of course, our imaginations have been so conditioned by economically determined spatial strictures that increasingly different people do in fact live next to each other and remain profoundly isolated."[2] The church is in need of people who will dare to talk to one an-

2. Jennings, *Christian Imagination*, 294.

other across racial and other lines. This kind of communication is not merely talk to hear oneself talk; it is not two or more people having a conversation and then disappearing into their respective lives, hardly ever to meet again. No, this kind of communication requires actually listening to the other person, uniting together in spiritual living, on a systematic basis within a faith community.

The primary listener plays an important role during cultural conflict. In some instances of cultural conflict, one party (or all parties) will be satisfied with a primary listener to the point of not feeling the need to carry on with the particular squabble. It is often powerful and healing to be in a safe setting to share concerns along with being heard. The primary listener helps create such a setting for the member or members experiencing distress. Listening is not easy and frequently not performed well. The primary listener should intentionally pay close attention to what is being said without offering any judgment, declarations, or verdicts about what really happened or what is going to happen next.

The Primary Facilitator

The primary facilitator serves as a neutral party without displaying preferential treatment. The primary facilitator should assign equal interest to all the parties in conflict, listening and speaking to one another about the issue(s) at hand. The primary facilitator's main goals should include securing an agreed-upon day, time, place for communication to occur for all those in conflict; helping ensure that everyone's concerns are conveyed and messages are heard, and making sure appropriate resources are available. People have different gifts within church community. It is important to identify people who can serve as a primary listener, and people who can serve as a primary facilitator. Rarely does one person serve well in two or more roles.

The Primary Negotiator

As a general rule, it is often best to resolve conflict at the lowest level. However, cultural conflict within the church can escalate to such a level that a primary negotiator is needed. Some cultural conflict within the church may necessitate more than one primary negotiator in order for all parties to feel supported. The primary negotiator(s) should have some knowledge of the context, respect from the parties involved, experience in mediation, and the skills and vision necessary to help achieve closure on difficult issues. While every church community should have more than one primary listener and more than one primary facilitator, it is not uncommon for there to be only one primary negotiator. In some cases, the primary negotiator may be a church member rather than the assigned pastor. In other cases, the primary negotiator may have to be recruited from outside of the congregation.

CHURCH LEADERSHIP DIPLOMACY METHODS IN TERRITORIAL CONFLICT

It is important for clergy to be willing and able to provide extensive pastoral leadership in their church setting. Clergy need to be equipped to navigate their congregations in the face of increasingly complex life circumstances and competing interests. Regardless of the church's structure, most parishioners will expect their pastor to guide them, especially in the midst of conflict. In some cross-racial pastoral ministry, pastoral leadership may be questioned, undervalued, and undermined simply on the basis of the pastor's ethnicity. Recommended church leadership diplomacy methods involve policies and procedures, rotation and shared access, and empowering the people.

In cross-racial pastoral ministry, it is best for clergypersons to embrace policies and procedures in the midst of territorial conflict. Clergypersons in cross-racial pastoral ministry are often examined through a powerful magnifying glass. People will quickly notice what type of pastoral diplomacy the clergyperson possesses (or lacks). Policies and procedures allow clergypersons to divert attention from themselves and thus allow for greater concentration on the congregation's rules and regulations. Policies and procedures can foster fewer allegations of favoritism and preferential treatment, fewer accusations of a dictatorial style of leadership, and more transparency in methods of operation.

In multicultural church ministry, rotation and shared access of facilities are most useful to help reduce territorial conflict. For instance, everyone associated with a multicultural ministry should get fair use of church property and resources. The shared usage of the church facility can occur on a weekly, monthly, quarterly, or monthly basis, just as long as the availability is fair to everyone. The agreed-upon rules should be clearly communicated, written down and made accessible in forms such as a website, trifold brochure, handbook, and posters, so that members will have a resource to guide them. Verbal agreements should not be the sole source of agreement because of the likelihood of misinterpretation, lack of communication, and the tendency of some members to leave the church.

CHURCH DIVERSITY ACTIVITIES AND IDENTITY CRISIS

In cross-racial pastoral ministry, some congregants will go through an identity crisis. It is important for the incoming clergyperson and the congregation to be mindful of how the membership self-identify. All congregations have a perception of themselves, and their level of accuracy varies. In many instances, the congregation's perception of itself differs from the community's view of the congregation. It is not necessary for all parties to agree on the congregations' role in the community. It is commendable when churches attempt objective examinations of themselves and consider the following three questions: What are we doing well? What are we not doing well? How do other people describe our congregation's presence in the community? These critical questions are not easy to answer, and the third question requires responses from people who are not associated with, or invested in, the congregation. It is typical for a congregation to undergo an identity crisis during cross-racial pastoral ministry and multicultural ministry. Congregations are generally good at remembering their past but can be reluctant to move into the present, and they may also refuse to adequately plan for their future. Church consultants Roy Oswald and Robert Friedrich Jr. observe that "every congregation has at least one myth about itself. . . . We all know how powerful myths are. Myths shape the way we perceive reality, and they tend to perpetuate themselves because people consistently live into the myths they believe about themselves. When a congregation's myth is too divorced from reality, there can be real pathology in that congregation."[3]

Church diversity activities, through education and recreation, can help congregations when they experience a crisis of identity. Education can occur through Bible studies, lectures, book clubs, mission trips, pulpit exchanges, choir exchanges, and workshops. The church community should offer educational opportunities on church diversity activities on a weekly, monthly, or quarterly basis in an attempt to accommodate the members' schedules and preferences in learning style. It is useful to highlight a few biblical examples of diversity among the people of God; I have selected three:

> And foreigners who bind themselves to the LORD to minister to him, to love the name of the LORD, and to be his servants, all who keep the Sabbath without desecrating it and who hold fast to my covenant—these I will bring to my holy mountain and give them joy in my house of prayer. Their burnt offerings and sacrifices will be accepted on my altar; for my house will be called a house of prayer for all nations. The Sovereign LORD declares—he who gathers the exiles of Israel: "I will gather still others to them besides those already gathered." (Isa 56:6–8)

> After this I looked, and there before me was a great multitude that no one could count, from every nation, tribe, people and language, standing before the throne

---

3. Oswald and Friedrich, *Discerning Your Congregation's Future*, 66.

and before the Lamb. They were wearing white robes and were holding palm branches in their hands. (Rev 7:9)

Have we not all one Father? Has not one God created us? Why then are we faithless to one another, profaning the covenant of our fathers? (Mal 2:10)

I recommend the following good resources that offer solutions and celebrate church diversity in the form of cross-racial ministry and multicultural ministry:

- *Relevant* magazine (www.relevantmagazine.com): see especially "What Diversity Should Look Like," by Matt Chandler (February 23, 2012) and "What Should Community Look Like?" by Adam Smith (August 7, 2008).

- *Unity in Christ* magazine (www.unityinchristmagazine.com): see especially "The Multiethnic Church Deepens the Meaning of Our Heavenly Adoption," by Robyn Afrik (June 22, 2013) and "Are Racially Diverse Churches Integrated?" by Erica Ryu Wong (October 28th, 2010).

- *The Christian Century* (www.christiancentury.org): see especially "Diverse Disciples," by Katherine Willis Pershey (July 6, 2011), "Poor and Unwanted," by Amy Frykholm (June 3, 2013), and "Lutherans Elect First Openly Gay Bishop," by John Dart (June 6, 2013).

Look for opportunities to increase church diversity through recreation; activities can include athletic events, retreats, and team-building, in addition to arts and crafts. I recommended activities and events such as the following:

1. Join a racially diverse church athletic league.[4]

2. Participate in a racially diverse church retreat focusing on spiritual leadership.[5]

4. Local YMCAs usually provide athletic leagues that are not restricted by race and gender. Additionally, some denominations offer leagues in various sports.

5. There are usually some religious facilities that offer specific retreat

3. Take part in a church mission trip to a different racial or cultural setting.

4. Participate in a school program that engages students who are culturally or racially different from the majority of the congregation's members.

The topic of diversity shapes our human landscape in profound ways. Diversity issues have been addressed in many famous movements, such as the civil rights movement, women's suffrage movement, and others. Too many people have been systematically taught and culturally instructed that people who are different are inferior or irrelevant. Those messages of antagonism are often directly or indirectly conveyed and interpreted through customs and traditions. There is nothing wrong with persons embracing their own personhood; however, there is something wrong when they embrace their own personhood at the expense or exclusion of others. Many of the movements toward greater diversity remind us of God's command in the book of Micah: "He has showed you, O man, what is good. And what does the LORD require of you? To act justly and to love mercy and to walk humbly with God" (6:8).

It is possible for church diversity to thrive, but it is amazing to observe the hermeneutical and exegetical gymnastics performed in order to avoid any major attempts at increasing diversity. Jesus preached to a diverse group of people as he was busy blessing the "poor and the poor in spirit" (Matt 5–7; Luke 6:19–21). His Sermon on the Mount highlights an example of the diversity congregations should actively seek to foster in their faith community. Cross-racial pastoral ministry and multicultural ministry are not the only two components of church diversity, but they are definitely two major components. Denominational leadership at every level should engage various aspects of church diversity. Why do congregations treat certain people unfairly? Sometimes it is merely a matter of priority. Time and energy are required of people of faith in order to achieve church diversity in their congregations.

---

programs.

Other priorities are usually more valued, such as the status of church finances, church attendance, and church buildings.

Christianity is a story. There are people living all over the world, in different countries and in various cultures, who believe that their story is included in Christianity's story. They are correct. Congregations need to convey the importance of all individuals in Christianity's story in a multifaceted way, such as through music, preaching, art, and literature. One way to help celebrate church diversity is through the sharing of people's stories. This involves educating, listening, and seeing the world from different perspectives and vantage points. It can be inspiring and therapeutic. People's stories are often complex and contradictory; yet, every person's story is extremely important. Ignoring or silencing a person's story will inhibit that person's growth and have effects that may be detrimental to her physical, mental, or spiritual health. There is power in every person's story, and congregations should nurture that concept of connecting their members' stories to the power of Jesus Christ.

It is important to understand that Christianity does not foster a homogeneous community. Christianity spans the globe. Differences of opinion on church diversity are fine, but it is better to be aware of influences upon one's ideas. One reason why people's ideas vary so widely is their level of experience and their understanding differ from others'. Solutions can be found that achieve a greater level of church diversity. Clergy and church leaders should be mindful that congregations should not be established for one particular type or kind of people.

In a nonthreatening environment, members of a congregation have opportunities to share joys and concerns about efforts toward church diversity. Asking questions is good and is often essential to any process that involves grappling with complex situations. The following questions should be included in serious dialogue:

1. In what ways could you help increase church diversity?

2. In what ways could you benefit from church diversity?

3. Why do you think church diversity is difficult to accomplish?

4. How do you think the congregation and surrounding community will respond to a greater level of church diversity?

5. Does the congregation currently have a formal relationship with other congregations of a different ethnicity?

6. What is it about church diversity that challenges you or makes you uncomfortable?

7. When do you think church diversity goes too far?

Congregations can learn some valuable lessons about racial integration from secular organizations that have made some progress, such as hospitals, law enforcement agencies, and schools, as well as many other institutions. A growing number of complex organizations have made cultural changes to their senior executive leadership. For example, American Express currently has an African-American CEO in the person of Kenneth Chenault; McDonald's currently has an African-American CEO in Don Thompson; Xerox currently has an African-American CEO in Ursula Burns; Harvard University has a female president, Catharine Gilpin Faust; the University of Virginia also has a female president, Teresa Ann Sullivan; and there are at least seven women currently governing U.S. states.

It is time for Christian denominations to take more leaps of faith in selecting senior pastoral leadership regardless of age, gender, or race. Within faith communities, one of the most important factors to be aware of is the power dynamic. While clergy definitely have power, the laity is not powerless. There is always a flow of power between the clergy and laity, which is negotiated through words and actions. Passivity does not help church diversity; dialogue rather than monologue is essential. People need to be able to share their thoughts without desperately seeking approval, which can get in the way of seeking solutions if it inhibits truth-telling. Possible solutions can emerge from people's honest cautions, concerns, and reservations. The correct knowledge, skills, and techniques can help in creating church diversity. Letters can also be helpful. I always appreciate a thoughtful letter written by someone who may have addressed the topic at hand or who may be able to offer valuable insight. One of the reasons why the Apostle Paul's letters are so popular is that they give the reader more access to the given situations. Along those lines, I offer the following two letters.

A LETTER TO THE CLERGY

Dear Pastor,

I pray God's blessings upon your pastoral ministry in church diversity. You will need to keep your hands steady on the gospel plow, because this kind of work is difficult; there are all kinds of challenges. Cross-racial pastoral ministry is demanding. It is not a pastoral ministry for clergy who thrive only on approval and praise from other people. It can make you feel lonely and isolated, because not many of your pastoral colleagues will be involved in this particular pastoral ministry. Disappointments are unavoidable and some conflict may become painfully personal. Pray often. Allow yourself to be the pastor your congregation needs despite the obvious racial and cultural differences. You will receive support from members whom you least expect to be supportive; in fact, you will be surprised by the many unexpected sources of support, both within the congregation and the surrounding community. Without a doubt, church diversity is significant.

My experience in cross-racial pastoral ministry has been one of the most important experiences in my life for God's glory. It has educated me, tested me, and spurred me to grow in ways I never imagined. The cross-racial pastoral ministry has helped me view the world differently, in a more critical and more creative manner. Concerning the critical, I realize there is a lot of work to be done to increase diversity within congregations. You will realize that most clergy do not participate in either cross-racial pastoral ministry or multicultural ministry. Try not to allow certain questions to haunt you: "Why isn't there more cross-racial pastoral ministry or multicultural ministry taking place?" Let that type of question help fuel your actions to build bridges rather than walls of division. I have encountered a great number of useless walls within church life that have stifled Christian growth.

Concerning the creative, I have dedicated my pastoral ministry to building bridges through church diversity. I am convinced that communities of faith need more bridges, which can help people connect with one another and God. Do not get intimidated or overwhelmed by the walls of division that humans have constructed out of fear, ignorance, and maliciousness. Direct more of your energy and attention to building bridges.

May God continue to bless you, your family, and your congregation. May you enjoy a humble confidence in your efforts to build bridges of partnerships between ethnicities and cultures. Rely on the Holy Spirit in the process. As always, include Jesus Christ, our Lord and Savior, in all of your pastoral endeavors, with special attention to a strategic consciousness for God's glory. Rest assured, God is with you in this particular vineyard.

A LETTER TO THE CHURCHES

Dear Congregation,

I pray God's blessings upon your church community's efforts toward greater diversity. Some of the most complex yet rewarding experiences are cross-racial pastoral ministry and multicultural ministry. Your congregation will encounter challenges different from any encountered before.

Church diversity is demanding. It questions preconceived notions about race and culture, up close and personal. You may be the only congregation in your surrounding area that exercises great intentionality in creating more diversity in church personnel. Not every congregation will appreciate or understand this type of commitment to diversity within the sacred space of your church's walls. Your lay leaders will need to be resilient. It is essential for clear messages about the value of all peoples to be celebrated through the entire year. Without a doubt, this ministry of church diversity is significant.

Remember to depend primarily on God in this process. Disappointments are unavoidable and some conflict may become painfully personal. Pray often. Allow yourself to be God's church despite some of the obvious racial and cultural differences among you. Support your pastor who was sent to you, and honor efforts toward greater church diversity. You are responsible to God and God's creation, God's people, and God's servant leader in the form of the pastor. You will be surprised by the sources of support from the congregation and surrounding community.

Cross-racial pastoral ministry and multicultural ministry will help you see the world in revelatory ways. In some ways, God's miraculous grace in the midst of once combative and now reconciled people will be a revelation to you. Additionally, your vision of God's kingdom will become larger in unexpected and unimaginable ways. Try not to allow questions of "progress" and "solidarity" haunt you, but rather let those types of questions help fuel your actions to build bridges between all Christians within faith communities, instead of walls of division. I am thankful to have encountered a great number of courageous laity who work to welcome all of God's creation within their faith community. During my years in cross-racial pastoral ministry, several laypersons have helped build bridges that I could not construct alone. That is why I can say that you are essential to God's church.

May God continue to bless you, your family, and your congregation. May you have faithful confidence in your efforts to build bridges of partnership between ethnicities and cultures. Rely on the Holy Spirit in the process. As always, call upon Jesus' resurrection power, in all of your congregational endeavors, with special attention to a global consciousness for God's glory. Rest assured, God is with you.

THE EXTRA MILES PLAN FOR MULTICULTURAL CHURCHES

There is generally a gap between theory and practice within any line of work; accordingly, there can be differences between Christianity as a religion, Christians as a particular people, and the Christian church as an institution. The "Extra Miles Plan" for multicultural congregations involves Christians trying their best to make the Christian church closely reflect Christianity—and thus make progress in their quest to follow Jesus Christ. There is value in study and training.

The church community, like most others, is influenced by print, visual, and audio media, which constitute a major part of what we see, hear, and even touch every day. In order for us to address the issue of the distribution of power, we cannot ignore the power of the media, which is so pervasive in our world today, for good or ill. One positive aspect of mass media is that it serves to let people of different cultures and nations see and hear how others live and what others' values are. It also projects which aspects of culture(s) are valued or not valued. An honest evaluation of a church's media displayed on their walls, website, and print documents, among other avenues, will reveal how they send subliminal messages about their level of diversity.

Christian churches need to use the various forms of media that will be affirming to all of God's children. Congregations need more images of diversity. Regardless of the dominant racial context of a congregation, various images of diversity should be displayed for all to view.

Substantial attention has not yet been given to the concept of inclusive congregations. Church leaders should obligate themselves to envision an inclusive future for their congregation. Too often, congregations are too fixated on their history without giving appropriate attention to their future. It is easy to focus more on the past, because the past is more familiar than the future.

During one of my cross-racial pastoral ministry moments, while eating a meal with one of the church leaders, he shared with me his appreciation for many aspects of my pastoral leadership, such as helping to strengthen the church's programs, adding new programs, providing pastoral care and counseling, and helping to bring in more church members. He further explained his excitement about my pastoral vision for an increasingly inclusive congregation that included strategically engaging the surrounding communities. It made an impact on me when he looked straight at me and stated that over his twenty years of being a member of that congregation he had not really noticed the empty pews and the lack of diversity. This was profound information. He continued to explain how he somehow held on too tightly to the congregation's past and, in doing so, he was prevented from giving adequate attention to the church's present status and future possibilities. The problem with congregations not envisioning an inclusive future is that it limits them today. There are numerous ways to honor history, tend to today, and intelligently anticipate the future.

The first step is prayer. It is good to envision an inclusive future by beginning with prayer. Prayer matters—individual prayers and collective prayers offered by all people within the faith community. Prayers should include asking God for wisdom, intervention, and guidance for the congregation's future. These prayers can take place in various settings, such as Bible study, children school, men's groups, women's groups, and worship services.

The second step is speaking. It is significant for the congregation to feel comfortable in making bold statements in relation to envisioning an inclusive future. These bold statements can help build confidence and an atmosphere of solidarity. It is one thing to think something but quite another to actually say something. Words matter. A person or group may have grand visions, but if they are not articulated, they will not have much value. Similar to most organizations, congregations need effective communication, an opportunity for respectful debate, adequate research, and solidarity in implementation.

The third step is writing. The Extra Miles process requires envisioning an inclusive future, articulating the vision in a faithful, confident manner, and writing it down. Writing matters. It helps inform and encourage the congregation's members, friends, and neighbors. The writing should be earnestly explored, examined, and reviewed before it is added to any publication, such as the church's newsletters, website, worship bulletins, or posters. It is normally best to publish short writings and not to think in terms of a thesis or dissertation. When it comes to the extra miles, brevity in writing is best. It should be considered a working document that can be revised rather than one that is "written in stone" like the Ten Commandments. Yet, the writing should be looked upon as a guidepost to work toward.

When a congregation envisions an inclusive future, it impacts almost every aspect of their faith community, including worship, mission outreach, and hiring. Worship should be examined for the messages being conveyed and who they are trying to reach. Another aspect is mission outreach, which should also be constructed so as to educate the congregation about their neighbors in need, as well as to develop partnerships. Mission outreach can be reviewed by asking such questions as these: How does the congregation make a difference in this community? If the congregation were removed, in what ways would it be missed by this community? Who are we helping with our mission outreach, and why? How does our envisioning an inclusive future impact our hiring process?

A GLOBAL GOD, A GLOBAL WORLD, A GLOBAL CHURCH

Implementing extra miles requires a view of a God that is global. A global perception of God helps actualize the connectivity to all of creation. It is difficult to follow Jesus Christ without tending to all God's children. God is creator of all peoples. Too often churches are extremely selective in terms of who they will accept as members. Jesus Christ calls us to be in relationship with people who are in prison, the ostracized and the poor, among others.

We live in a global world, especially in the U.S., where people from different cultures live next door to one another, work together, interact with one another, and, increasingly, marry one another. Organizations are becoming more inclusive; these include medical facilities, educational institutions, law enforcement, entertainment, professional athletics, and others. In most public spaces across the United States, especially in cities, there is noticeable diversity, with the exception of Christian churches. Why are most churches not as diverse as the businesses and organizations next door to them?

A global church should reflect a global God who created a global world. A global church reflects diversity at every level within congregational life—worship, education, staff, community partners, members, music, media, mission outreach, and art. Are more congregations willing to become a global church? If not, why not? Are more pastors willing to help lead their congregations toward becoming globally conscious? If not, why not? A global church does not happen on its own, without the intentionality of church leaders. A global church is not fixated upon itself. It is not solely focused upon its members' joys and concerns. It exercises an inward introspection and outward perspective. A global church pays careful attention to the miraculous ways God's presence is moving across ethnic lines and geographical boundaries. We serve a global God. Let us not attempt to confine or restrict God.

There are a variety of ways a pastor, member, and congregation can measure their progress toward becoming a global church. One way is to invite a church consultant on diversity matters to give an audit on the congregation's inclusivity. Another option is to have a combination of pastors and laity with experience and expertise lead a series of workshops discussing how to improve a faith community's global consciousness. A pastor and congregation should ask themselves the following questions:

1. How do the sermons reflect a global God, a global world, and a global church?

2. How does the worship experience reflect a global God, a global world, and a global church?

3. How do my relationships reflect a global God, world, and church?

4. How do my preaching, teaching, and counseling reflect a global God, world, and church?

5. How do my partnerships within the surrounding community reflect a global God, world, and church?

6. In what ways am I (or we) not reflecting a global God, a global world, and a global church?

7. How can I (or we) improve to reflect a global God, world, and church?

8. Are there global aspects of my pastoral ministry?

9. What message(s) about a global God, a global world, and a global church might we be sending the younger generation(s) of our faith community?

10. In what ways does our congregation reflect a global God, world, and church?

These questions can be modified for certain groups within the congregation. They can be given to the congregation on paper or via email with the expectation of a written response, or they can be shared in verbal discussions during various church meetings. Practical theology requires *experience, exploration, reflection, and response.*[6] Recommendations are rooted in experience and questions formulated to encourage exploration. The questions are intended to help faith communities have an honest dialogue about their status, their ability, and their willingness to move forward into serving a global God. We live in a global world, as a global church, one that should reflect love, grace, respect, forgiveness, and reconciliation.

6. Lartey, "Practical Theology as Theological Form," in Woodward and Pattison, *Pastoral and Practical Theology*, 130.

Bibliography

"ABHMS-endorsed Military Chaplain Makes Women's History." *American Baptist News Service*, March 14th, 2013. http://www.abc-usa. org/2013/03/14/abhms-endorsed-military-chaplain-makes-womens-history/.

Andrews, Dale P. *Practical Theology for Black Churches: Bridging Black Theology and African American Folk Religion*. Louisville: Westminster John Knox, 2002.

Bantum, Brian. *Redeeming Mulatto: A Theology of Race and Christian Hybridity*. Waco: Baylor University Press, 2010.

Berkley, James D., ed. *Leadership Handbook of Outreach and Care*. Grand Rapids: Baker, 1997.

Blake, John. "Why Many Americans Prefer Their Sundays Segregated." *CNN. Com*, http://www.cnn.com/2008/LIVING/wayoflife/08/04/segregated. sundays/index.html.

Boisen, Anton T. *Problems in Religion and Life: A Manual for Pastors*. New York: Abingdon-Cokesbury, 1946.

Bonhoeffer, Dietrich. *Selected Writings*. Edited by Edwin Robertson. New York: HarperCollins, 1995.

Brown, Vicki. "Lead Women Pastors Make Recommendations." The United Methodist Church, General Board of Higher Education and Ministry, August 1, 2011. http://www.gbhem.org/article/lead-women-pastors-make-recommendations#.UbupjSLD8iQ.

Browning, Don S. *A Fundamental Practical Theology: Descriptive and Strategic Proposals*. Minneapolis: Fortress, 1991.

Byassee, Jason. "Team Players: What Do Associate Pastors Want?" *The Christian Century*, January 24, 2006, 18.

Cambell, Alastair. "The Nature of Practical Theology." In *The Blackwell Reader in Pastoral and Practical Theology*, edited by James Woodward and Stephen Pattison, 77–88. Oxford: Blackwell, 2000.

Carter, Judith Corbett. "Gender Differences and Leadership Styles in a Non-Secular Setting." *Open Journal of Leadership* 1 (2012) 1–4.

Clinebell, Howard. *Basic Types of Pastoral Care and Counseling: Resources for the Ministry of Healing and Growth*. Nashville: Abingdon, 1984.

Conde-Frazier, Elizabeth. "A Spiritual Journey toward Peaceful Living." In *Choosing Peace through Daily Practices*, edited by Ellen Ott Marshall, 158–85. Cleveland: Pilgrim, 2005.

Cone, James. *The Cross and the Lynching Tree*. Maryknoll, NY: Orbis, 2013.

———. *For My People: Black Theology and the Black Church*. Maryknoll, NY: Orbis, 1984.

———. *Speaking the Truth*. Maryknoll, NY: Orbis, 1999.

De La Torre, Miguel A., ed. *AAR Career Guide for Racial and Ethnic Minorities in the Profession*. Atlanta: AAR, 2006. https://www.aarweb.org/publications/arr-career-guide-racial-and-ethnic-minorities-profession.

Dougherty, Kevin D. "How Monochromatic Is Church Membership? Racial-Ethnic Diversity in Religious Community." *Sociology of Religion* 64 (2003) 65–85.

Douglas, Kelly Brown. *The Black Christ*. Maryknoll, NY: Orbis, 1994.

Ebenstein, Avraham. "The 'Missing Girls' of China and the Unintended Consequences of the One Child Policy." *Journal of Human Resources* 45.1 (2010) 87–115. Online: http://pluto.huji.ac.il/~ebenstein/Ebenstein_OneChildPolicy_2010.pdf.

Emerson, Michael O., with Rodney M. Woo. *People of the Dream: Multiracial Congregations in the United States*. Princeton: Princeton University Press, 2006.

Episcopal News Service. "Episcopal Church Leaders Endorse Comprehensive Immigration Reform Legislation." October 18, 2005. http://archive.episcopalchurch.org/3577_68618_ENG_HTM.htm.

Evangelical Lutheran Church in America. "Toward Compassionate, Just, and Wise Immigration Reform." Social policy resolution adopted by the Church Council of the Evangelical Lutheran Church in America, November 2009. http://resources.elca.org/Social_Issues-Toward_Compassionate_Just_Wise_Immigration_Reform.html.

Fedler, Kyle D. *Exploring Christian Ethics: Biblical Foundations for Morality*. Louisville: Westminster John Knox, 2006.

Felder, Cain Hope. *Troubling Biblical Waters*. Maryknoll, NY: Orbis, 1990.

Fowler, James W. "Faith Development Theory and the Challenges of Practical Theology." In *Developing a Public Faith: New Directions in Practical Theology; Essays in Honor of James W. Fowler*, edited by Richard R. Osmer and Friedrich L. Schweitz, 229–50. St. Louis: Chalice, 2003.

Guilmoto, Christophe Z. "Sex Ratio Imbalance in Asia: Trends, Consequences, and Policy Responses." Fourth Asia Pacific Conference on Reproductive and Sexual Health and Rights, United Nations Population Fund, October 29, 2007. Online: http://tinyurl.com/4ldcpgd. Referenced in Mara Hvistendahl, *Unnatural Selection: Choosing Boys Over Girls, and the Consequences of a World Full of Men*. New York: Public Affairs, 2011.

Harris, Hamil R., and Michelle Boorstein. "At D.C.'s First Baptist Church, a Dismal Parting with Its First Black Pastor." *Washington Post*, May 1, 2013. http://www.washingtonpost.com/local/at-dcs-first-baptist-church-a-dismal-parting-with-its-first-black-pastor/2013/05/01/9397e352-b280-11e2-9a98-4be1688d7d84_story.html.

Heitink, Gerben. *Practical Theology: History, Theory, Action Domains; Manual for Practical Theology*. Translated by Reinder Bruinsma. Grand Rapids: Eerdmans, 1999.

Jennings, Willie James. *The Christian Imagination: Theology and the Origins of Race*. New Haven: Yale University Press, 2011.

Keller, Rosemary Skinner, ed. *Spirituality and Social Responsibility: Vocational Vision of Women in the United Methodist Tradition*. Nashville: Abingdon, 1993.

Lartey, Emmanuel Y. *In Living Color*. 2nd ed. London: J. Kingsley, 2004.

Law, Eric H. F. *The Wolf Shall Dwell with the Lamb*. St. Louis: Chalice, 1993.

Lehmann, Paul L. *Ethics in a Christian Context*. Louisville: Westminster John Knox, 2003.

Marable, Manning, et al., eds. *Freedom on My Mind: The Columbia Documentary History of the African American Experience*. New York: Columbia University Press, 2003.

Marshall, Ellen Ott, ed. *Choosing Peace through Daily Practices*. Cleveland: Pilgrim, 2005.

McBeth, H. Leon. *The Baptist Heritage: Four Centuries of Baptist Witness*. Nashville: Broadman, 1987.

McNerthney, Casey. "Number of Female Police Chaplains Increasing: More Women Reaching Out during a Time of Need." *Seattle PI*, August 7, 2007. http://www.seattlepi.com/local/article/Number-of-female-police-chaplains-increasing-1245958.php.

Mirrer, Louise, and William B. Harrison, Jr. *The New York Amsterdam News*. October 7–March 5, 2005.

"Mount Angel Seminary Educates Catholic Women." *Catholic Sentinel*, October 18, 2011. http://www.catholicsentinel.org/main.asp?SectionID=4&SubSectionID=29&ArticleID=16449&TM=48842.8.

Norwood, Frederick A. *The Story of American Methodism*. Nashville: Abingdon, 1974.

Oates, Wayne E. *New Dimensions in Pastoral Care*. Philadelphia: Fortress, 1970.

Oswald, Roy M., and Robert E. Friedrich, Jr. *Discerning Your Congregation's Future: A Strategic and Spiritual Approach*. Herndon, VA: Alban Institute, 1996.

Pattison, Stephen. *The Challenge of Practical Theology: Selected Essays*. London: J. Kingsley, 2007.

Pattison, Stephen, and James Woodward. "An Introduction to Pastoral and Practical Theology." In *The Blackwell Reader in Pastoral and Practical Theology*, edited by James Woodward and Stephen Pattison, 1–19. Oxford: Blackwell, 2000.

Pohlmann, Marcus D., ed. *African American Political Thought*. 6 vols. New York: Routledge, 2003.

BIBLIOGRAPHY

Pryde, Paul. "Investing in People: A New Approach to Job Creation." In *African American Political Thought*, edited by Marcus D. Pohlmann, 4:303–5. New York: Routledge, 2003.

Pui-lan, Kwok. *Introducing Asian Feminist Theology*. Cleveland: Pilgrim, 2000.

Raboteau, Albert J. *Slave Religion: The Invisible Institution*. Oxford: Oxford University Press, 2004.

Rah, Soong-Chan. *Many Colors: Cultural Intelligence for a Changing Church*. Chicago: Moody, 2010.

Robertson, Campbell. "Bishops Criticize Tough Alabama Immigration Law." *New York Times*, August 13, 2011. http://www.nytimes.com/2011/08/14/us/14immig.html?pagewanted=&_r=0.

Schmidt, Jean Miller. *Grace Sufficient: A History of Women in American Methodism, 1760–1968*. Nashville: Abingdon, 1999.

Sernett, Milton C. *African American Religious History: A Documentary Witness*. Durham: Duke University Press, 1999.

Shawchuck, Norman, and Roger Heuser. *Leading the Congregation: Caring for Yourself while Serving the People*. Nashville: Abingdon, 2010.

Smith, Huston. *The World's Religions*. New York: HarperCollins, 1991.

Smith, Robert London, Jr. *From Strength to Strength: Shaping a Black Practical Theology for the Twenty-First Century*. New York: P. Lang, 2007.

Stevenson-Moessner, Jeanne. *Prelude to Practical Theology: Variations on Theory and Practice*. Nashville: Abingdon, 2008.

Swinton, John, and Harriet Mowat. *Practical Theology and Qualitative Research*. London: SCM, 2006.

Teresa of Avila, Saint. *Interior Castle*. Translated and edited by E. Allison Peers. New York: Dover, 2007.

Thomas, James S. *Methodism's Racial Dilemma*. Nashville: Abingdon, 1992.

Viau, Marcel. *Practical Theology: A New Approach*. Translated by Robert Hurley and Chantal Tanguay. Leiden: Brill, 1999.

Vitello, Paul. "Riverside Church Pastor Resigns after Nine Months." *New York Times*, June 30, 2009. http://cityroom.blogs.nytimes.com/2009/06/30/riverside-church-pastor-resigns-after-2-months/.

Willimon, William. *Pastor: The Theology and Practice of Ordained Ministry*. Nashville: Abingdon, 2002.

Wimberly, Edward P. *African American Pastoral Care*. Cleveland: Pilgrim, 2006.

Winseman, Albert L. "Race and Religious Leadership." *Gallup.com*, March 9, 2004. http://www.gallup.com/poll/10921/Race-Religious-Leadership.aspx.

Wiseman, Alison. "Women Increasing in Numbers at Southeastern Seminary." *Baptist Press*, May 7, 1997. http://www.bpnews.net/bpnews.asp?id=3298.

Woodward, James, and Stephen Pattison, eds. *The Blackwell Reader in Pastoral and Practical Theology*. Oxford: Blackwell, 2000.

Zikmund, Barbara Brown, et al. "Women, Men and Styles of Clergy Leadership." *The Christian Century*, May 6, 1998. http://hirr.hartsem.edu/bookshelf/clergywomen_summary.html.